Making Money, Not Just A Living

by

Les Jansson

&

Don MacLaren

ISBN 978-0-9797605-0-1

Published by: ~ Max and Company ~
Point Lookout, New York

Printed in the United States of America
Printed on Recycled Paper
Published February 2009

Dedication

To my wife, Ann, who has supported me throughout all my adventures and to my son, Les, who helped me succeed in many of my businesses. Their love and respect have helped me to gain success and inner peace.

Table of Contents

Dedication.. 3
Table of Contents.. 5
Chapter 1 The Story That Changed My Life........................ 1
Chapter 2 Blind Ambition 20
Chapter 3 Do Your Homework... 39
Chapter 4 Every Door Opens Another Door 59
Chapter 5 Life's An Adventure 82
Chapter 6 Be A Good Card Player..................................... 89
Chapter 7 Looking Outside the Box 105
Chapter 8 Be a Good Listener 129
Chapter 9 Consultants 141
Chapter 10 Long-Term Goals... 150
Chapter 11 Position Yourself 158
Chapter 12 The Forest and the Trees 161
Chapter 13 Be on the Right Street and Walk.................... 167
Chapter 14 Seminar Selling... 173
Chapter 15 Live Below Your Means 186

Chapter 1

The Story That Changed My Life

At the age of thirty-five, I was always making a good living with my businesses, jobs, careers, and adventures, but I was never making real money or getting to the next level.

I felt frustrated watching other people succeeding, while I seemed to be sitting on the sidelines. What were their secrets? What were their strategies? What would it take to be successful? What would it take to achieve inner peace?

Finally, by sheer chance, I met a gentleman who would become my boss, but, more importantly, he would alter my life. He not only revolutionized my thoughts, but acted as my mentor on the road to success. He changed my life by changing the way I thought. He gave me some lessons that helped me find the strategies to becoming successful.

What I came to learn after age thirty-five took me from a $60,000 a year income to making $600,000 a year and operating a multi-million dollar business.

I believe we can influence each other to accomplish something great. I believe one or more of the lessons in this book will help you to be successful, whether in business, career, personal attitudes, or your relationships.

There are different measures of success. One measurement is money. Another measurement is respect from others. Another measurement is your accomplishments. Whether you are making $50,000 and you want to make $100,000 or you are making $500,000 and want to make $5 million a year or you want to be the most respected person in your field, the lessons in this book will help you create a path and a plan to find success or your new level of accomplishments. Wouldn't it be great to be respected and be financially rewarded at the same time? You can be a champion in many different ways.

Success is not accidental. We can change our circumstances and change the outcome of our lives.

- I believe there is a higher level of success waiting for you. Are you willing to do what it takes to get to the next level?

Some people are afraid of success because they fear failing. Fear of this or that holds too many people back from accomplishing something greater. They may be afraid of the risks, responsibilities, losing investment money, an unexpected catastrophe, and a million other reasons for not becoming successful. This book is about learning to think with new perspectives and see with new eyes that the world has millions of opportunities around you. Mistakes, problems, some poor judgment and choices, and some failures will happen. They are inevitable for all of us. And if you are prone to making mistakes, it would be wise to have consultants and lawyers as part of your team to protect yourself. However, all the problems that come along should be considered "minor" compared to your accomplishments, once you have revolutionized your way of thinking. I want to tell the story about what helped me to see the world differently.

I had been working several years on Long Island as an entrepreneur in the automobile insurance company salvage business. That meant I would buy cars sold by insurance companies at auctions that had sustained damage caused by collisions or theft. I would then resell the cars. The business does not sound glamorous as compared to other people's careers or to someone working in Hollywood. I am glad I was working there because that one career changed my whole life.

From my previous auto body shop business, I knew how to repair damaged cars, either for a customer or for resale. I accomplished those goals in a couple of days and always at a profit. I had become successful on a small scale, but I did not know how to get to the next level financially. Buying and reselling cars from insurance companies without repairing them was the better business model.

While at an insurance company auction, I happened to meet another gentleman in the same business whom I will call Joe. From conversations with those at the auctions, I knew that Joe had a similar business as mine in the Bronx and he was known to be rather successful. Although about ten years younger than me, he had established himself as a key player in this business.

He came up to me and introduced himself. After we shook hands, he went on to tell me, "I've been watching you for a while. You know exactly how to pick the cars. You bid exactly the right wholesale money on the car. I can do this too, but my problem is that I really don't have the time to do it anymore. I'd be interested in hiring you as a buyer."

"I'm flattered, but I have my own business on Long Island. But thanks for the offer," I said. We chatted for a few minutes and then we went our separate ways.

As I drove back to my business that same day, I had no idea I was about to run into serious trouble. While I had been busy starting my auto reselling business, I had never followed up on getting the right permits for the location I was renting. At $100 per month, who cares?

Whether by coincidence or divine fate, a representative from the town came into my office shortly after I got back. He gave me the bad news, "If you don't get these cars off this site and close down this operation in thirty days, we're going to put you out of business. You'll be facing a fine of $5,000 a day."

After he left, I only needed two minutes to know what I had to do. I knew I could not afford to buy the land or to obtain the proper permits quickly.

I might have gone into depression thinking about losing my business, except I remembered Joe's offer. I stopped what I was doing to think, *Joe just offered me a position to become a buyer for him! Is that coincidence or what? That's pretty interesting. He is going to pay me to go out and spend his company's money. I'll be car shopping with Joe's checkbook. This could be a good adventure!*

I always looked forward to finding new career adventures. Now forced out of my business by circumstances that may have gotten out of control, I called Joe and set up an appointment to meet him. At the meeting, we struck up a deal. Before leaving, I explained to him, "I'll be back to work for you in three weeks. I have to close down my operation."

The timing could not have been better. I began as a buyer for his business in the Bronx. The company was only in business about five years, owned by Joe and his brother, and it already had about 50 employees. Both brothers were very sharp, though I came to think that Joe was more business-oriented than his brother. But his brother had a great way with the employees and they showed him great respect, so the business operated with a great team spirit.

As I worked with Joe, I watched how he ran that business. Joe turned out to be the kind of businessman who could teach me how to be successful.

Almost every Monday, Joe and I would spend the day together. I'm sure he heard some insights from me. But I learned far more about business than I ever learned on my own. He was a great mentor. I was beginning to learn his knowledge and business methodologies.

I had been working there one year when tragedy would suddenly strike.

Joe had decided to go on his first vacation in four years. He asked me if I could come in at night after buying at the auctions. I had very little to do with the inside operations, but I agreed to come in when he wanted me there to help his brother get the paperwork in order and close out the day.

The company was set up with two departments: the

parts and the repairable autos for resale. Joe oversaw the whole business, while his brother focused on the department that sold the used parts. In my section, we only had four people, but we were responsible for bringing in fifty percent of the profits because Joe and I had to know how to bid the right price on the right cars so they could be sold for a profit.

While Joe was on vacation, I came into the office at the end of the day to check on things for him, to help his brother count the money, and to see the day's results. By the time I finished, it was around 7 P.M. His brother and I only had to wait for a driver who had made a late delivery of some cars and had to make his way back through the New York City traffic. Since the yard was located in the Bronx, I faced a long drive from the Bronx to my home in Massapequa on Long Island.

His brother said, "Les, the driver will be here in a few minutes. Listen, you better get home. Your wife probably has dinner on the table." He smiled and waved at me to go ahead and leave.

I called my wife to let her know my plans, "I'm leaving the yard. If the traffic's not too bad, I should be home for dinner in about half an hour."

"Okay, I'll have dinner ready," she said.

I got in my car and drove out of the yard. As I stopped to look both ways before entering the street, I saw an old Chevy parked on the street to the left with some people in it. I thought nothing of it and went on home.

The next morning I got a call from a fellow buyer who told me not to go to any auctions that day. I was shocked to hear the news: Joe's brother and two other employees had been shot and killed ten minutes after I had left. I felt terrible for Joe and his family because his brother was a great person and a great loss to those who knew him.

The police investigation finally led them to a former employee and some of his friends who had come in to rob the place, knowing there would be cash on hand from the cars sold, but the thieves must have panicked and killed anyone who could identify them as former employees.

I was lucky. I missed being killed by ten minutes.

Joe closed the business for a week in observance of his brother's death. After that, Joe kept operating the business and took over his brother's role. I stayed on. That second year with Joe became important in my life because I began learning even more about being successful.

I had learned some valuable lessons in the first year when Joe and I would spend every Monday or every other Monday traveling together to the automobile auctions. I had already begun applying his formulas on every facet of his business. Whenever I spent time with Joe, he shared his business ideas. Interestingly enough, what he said turned into lessons that I needed to learn. In this book, we will delve into the ideas passed on from Joe and a lot of good ideas that I have learned since. During the second year, Joe mostly ran the whole business and I was more on my own, using the lessons I had learned.

- Lesson: Make business into a game.

- Lesson: Every business has a plan and formulas.

"Les, business is like a game," Joe said. "In every game, you have to know the rules and then you have to outsmart your opponent. If you play the game well, the money will follow. But don't set getting the money as the priority."

- Lesson: Don't be concerned with the money.

- Lesson: The business principles that you will learn in this book are powerful because knowing what to do results in bringing in the money.

Joe told me that they had the money when it came to buying at the auctions. He did not want me to worry about writing the checks. He trusted my judgment to buy the right cars. He wanted me to concentrate on the right cars, and not to worry about anything else.

If I bought one car too many, we were not going to worry about it. He saw the bigger picture. They could always sell a car another week. I knew a lot of our competitors were small entrepreneurs, so they would be worried about every dollar and that could weaken the way they would bid.

"We'll take care of the money," Joe assured me.

I knew they did not have an endless supply of money or maybe they did, but, whenever they needed money, they could lay their hands on it.

Joe wanted me to be out there with a clear mind, which made me think better and to focus on making better buys at the auctions. In my own business, I used to worry whether I could afford to buy two, five, or ten cars. When I sold a car, I had the worry of waiting for the checks to clear. Of course, I always made sure I never wrote someone a check at the auctions that wouldn't clear because my own reputation had to be impeccable at the auctions.

I knew in the business I owned that I had been limited by the amount of space I could rent and limited in the amount of money I had to bid at the auctions. However, I knew I did have a lot of talent. Working with Joe, I could expand on that talent.

My relationship with Joe raises some important questions between you and the people you work for or the people who work for you.

- How many employees get that kind of trust from their employer that Joe gave me?

- How many employers trust their employees?

- How many employers trust their employees as equally as they trust themselves?

- How many times does an employer help an employee expand his talents?

These questions raise substantial issues that can make a big difference in how well a company grows. Companies are essentially employees of various talents who relate to themselves and to the customers.

The response time in getting to a customer and the quality of taking care of a customer can make a company successful or not.

- Small, non-franchised businesses have a high rate of failure and statistically only about 3 out of 100 businesses are still viable three years later.

As we drove along one day, Joe shared one of his ideas that became another principle for me. Restaurants probably experience one of the highest rates of business failures. Let's take one French restaurant. You know that place because you take your wife or someone there on very special occasions. It's a little expensive. But you want to go there. You drive up to the restaurant in your car. The parking attendant comes to your door and opens it. He says, 'Hi, Mr. Jansson. Glad to see you again.' You feel good already. You walk in. The place is clean as a whistle. The maitre d' knows your name and finds *your* table because he knows that's where you always like to sit. The silverware is spotless. You don't have to wipe off the soap spots on the silverware with your napkin. You like the French onion soup with the cheese on top and the garlic twist. You always remember that and everybody orders it. It's exactly the way you remembered it. You have a great meal. Normally, you spend fifty bucks for you and your wife. This bill is eighty-five. Maybe you knew you paid a little too much, but you always felt good. And you'll go back. You'll tell your friends what a great place it is.

"For every ten small restaurants that open around the country, there's only about one still in business three years later. But this restaurant that is special has been there for twenty years. The owner may not be there all the time, but he has a great staff. The owner and the manager have taught everyone to watch over the little things and make sure everything is perfect. Every employee has to be attentive to the customer and keep coming over to them to ask if everything is all right. The owners and managers who fail typically fail because they are not attentive to the little things. It's the accumulation of the little things done consistently well that makes a business a success.

The same is true for franchises. If you walk into a McDonald's or Taco Bell and order a meal, you have confidence that you get the same quality all the time. There is a manager making sure every employee there is dressed properly. It may sound ridiculous, but, if you walked into a franchise restaurant and saw everybody walking around in dirty uniforms, the kitchen staff was not using plastic gloves to prepare the food, or you saw a mouse, you would not want to go back. A company makes impressions with all the small details.

Joe told me once that he would deliberately call me from outside to see how long it took the counter people to answer the phone. He wanted the phone answered in two or three rings. That's the importance he placed on taking care of the customer. I began learning that he had the smallest details down to a science.

- Lesson: Everything you do in your business, you have to do at 110% to beat your competitors. In other words, the 110% effort means making hundreds of improvements in small ways that will "sell you" to your customers better than what your competition offers.

Grading a business is much different than what we

were taught about getting grades in school. A 65 or 70 grade in school means you just managed to pass. In business, a 65 or 70 means you haven't started. Running a business where you might get a grade of eighty-five percent is not good enough. Eighty-five percent in business means you're going to be out of business. If you operate at a hundred percent in business, it's still not good enough.

Business is always changing. You have to do 110% every day. That means every day in every way—and never miss a beat. To make sure you're always doing 110%, look at all your long-term goals. For example, maybe fish is no longer good on that restaurant menu. Maybe you have to change something else on the menu. Maybe you have to put on the menu a different type of meat. A good business person will look at the long-term goals. Now is that difficult to do? Yes, it's difficult to do, but look at the satisfaction. All the other nine restaurants on that block went out of business, but your restaurant is still there.

That 110% story became the missing link for me between one level of success and the next higher level. At first, I didn't think much of it. But the more I thought about it, the more I understood the effort it would take and what I had to do.

That story about always having a business working at 110% stuck with me.

I learned from Joe it did not matter what kind of business it was. You could be opening a restaurant, an auto parts, or an insurance company. What counted was playing the game at 110% every day of the week.

- Lesson: If you get the game (principles) right, the money will follow. (You can put that on my tombstone.)

I started analyzing my own life because I had already been in lots of businesses. By the age of 35, I was one of those people who had hopped between 20 jobs and businesses. These career adventures were okay, but nothing great. That little 110% story made me think where I was.

I thought, *I've already owned a successful auto body business and proven to be the most productive and profitable auto painter at a large California dealership. I may be a little smarter than the average worker in a lot of skills. When I've done things, I've always done that 110% thing with my skills. And as far as being an employee, everybody wants to hire me. But in business, if I was going to the next level, I was going to have to use this new knowledge to expand my level of success.*

Lesson: The right tools (knowledge) are more important than the investment money.

A year after his brother had been killed and two years after I had been working with Joe, I made the decision to go back into my own business doing the same work.

I opened my company with my own savings. I liked to say I went from "zero dollars" and took it to $4,000,000 in sales in two years. Part of how I got there are other lessons I'll be sharing.

To start out, I did not have an endless amount of money, but I had accumulated new tools (knowledge), which I had come to learn were just as important as the amount of investment money. This book will take you through the steps to learn the tools and the principles that you need to apply.

- Lesson: Knowledge is more important than the capital because with the right knowledge you can grow a business and ultimately bring in the capital.

If someone came to me and said, "I want to start a business," my first question would likely be, "How good is your knowledge about that business?" Whether the person has enough capital is further down my list of questions. I like to repeat: knowledge is more important than the amount of your financial backing. If you don't have the knowledge about what you're doing in that business, you'll get overwhelmed, waste the investment money, and very likely be out of business.

Doctors, lawyers, and other professional people are good examples of those who have to gain a lot of knowledge before they can make the money in their profession and become successful.

Whenever we drove together, I listened to Joe share his ideas and philosophy because that meant I was learning something. He knew how to think like a business leader.

Our age difference didn't matter: I was 35 and he was 25. Most young men his age may not be so driven or focused about business. He was already married and had one priority: to run a successful business. Since he had proven his success, I came to trust what he said.

- Lesson: Don't start a business unless you have the right tools, especially the right knowledge.

I knew I could have continued working with Joe as long as I wanted. I *knew myself* well enough to know that I always had a lot of ambition. But ambition and drive are not enough to be successful.

You need all the other tools when you go into business. If you don't have the tools, you will be just another good employee.

When I look back at my career at that point, I realized I had jumped into my careers and businesses without having all the tools. I had only part of the tools, that's why I was only partly successful.

What I learned from Joe I felt was the equivalent of getting a diploma in business. That's how important those two years with Joe were for me. I am hopeful that by the time you finish reading this book you will have the principles that will help you to a new level in your business, your career, and your relationships.

- Lesson: A student's grades may be a poor guide as to whether that person will be successful.

I struggled with learning difficulties when I was in school. All the other students passed their tests with high scores, while I could hardly pass a test. Once I became an adult, I found out my problem in school had something to do with "instant recall." I could not recall information as well as my classmates.

Also, I was not as good as the other students at taking tests, but I learned early as a child that *I could still accomplish things, if I applied myself.* In the world of business, I learned to apply myself and to outperform my former classmates, proving that the good "test takers" in school were not necessarily successful out in the real world.

After I left my job with Joe, I was back in my own business with a new set of eyes. I felt ready to start over because I had all new the tools that I had learned from working with Joe in his business.

I knew I had to forget about just making a living. A living I could make, whether it be $50,000 or $100,000. And that idea relates to the book's title: *Making Money, Not Just A Living*.

I was now about to go to the next level to make something great happen with the new tools I had obtained. Also, I felt I had obtained my "Diploma in Business," thanks to Joe.

Chapter 2

Blind Ambition

Another thing I found in the business world that is required to be successful is what I call Blind Ambition.

The fire of ambition cannot be on-again and off-again. It takes a consistent fire that burns on the good days and the bad days. On the bad days when things seem to be going against you, that's when your blind ambition should keep you going strong so you can overcome everything and not be defeated.

Anyone who does not have the strong fire of blind ambition will always have excuses as to what went wrong and what kept him or her from being successful.

- Lesson: Each person needs to find a fire of blind ambition inside and keep the fire alive to be successful.

Since I could not be a good student, I compensated by learning to work hard and to excel at making things work better in my life.

As a child, my parents had me take piano lessons. I liked music and sang in the choir in church, but I never liked learning to play the piano. I admit there was no blind ambition in me to learn the piano.

When I was fifteen, my cousin Fred came by and put a guitar in my hands. He said, "I'm going on vacation. You can have my guitar while I'm away. See if you like playing it." He showed me a couple of chords to play. After he left, I started playing and singing.

When he came back two weeks later, I almost had a band put together. The guitar became my instrument. From that moment on, I developed a blind ambition to play the guitar and sing.

I excelled at ambition as a child. As an example of that, I was unlike most children because I had three paper routes. One was not enough. The two extra routes meant more spending money and more snacks for me to buy.

I made money going around cutting lawns too. After walking to a lot of homes, I thought, *Why should I go all around the area to cut lawns when I could cut everybody's lawn on the block and give them a price break for saving me travel time?* I ended up cutting everyone's lawn on one block. At an early age, I was already trying to improve my business.

With the guitar in my hands, I thought, *If I learn the guitar, maybe I could entertain the other kids.* That took me in a track for many years of trying to be a rock star with a band. I did make a living and had some minor success for some 12 years. I loved entertaining because I got a great feeling connecting to the audience.

I was always learning blind ambition at an early age because I pushed myself to be better and to find ways to increase my income.

Blind ambition and drive I did have. Once out of school, that fire within me had helped me to accomplish so much more. However, I still had more to accomplish in life.

As I began later in life consulting with people about success and their careers, people would say, "I want to start a business, but, before I do, I want to take my two weeks vacation." Or, they would say, "I'm going to buy a new car and then open a business." As I saw it, they were expressing a fear that, after they got into business, they would not have any money to do anything. I considered that a wrong attitude. By having a successful business, you will be set free and find personal and financial freedom.

If you are thinking about leaving one job or career

and going into business for yourself, my advice is to live frugally. You have to be willing to commit your money to the new adventure and be willing to give up the luxury of a vacation or a new car. That new car might cost you $25,000. However, you may need that $25,000 as your extra capital and reserve. Don't think about your luxuries. Focus on having as much money and credit available to invest back into the business.

Running a new business will likely require you to make sacrifices and to forgo luxuries and pleasure for a while. In other words, a new business may require you to sacrifice in new ways.

- Lesson: The people who want the greater success are the ones who have the blind ambition and drive, and who make the sacrifices to accomplish their goals.

On the negative side of ambition, I have seen successful people leave a path of destruction behind them. With blind ambition, you do not want to alienate people working with you. You want to be respected. Developing strong friendships within the business community does help. The more respect you gain the more you can accomplish. Cooperation breeds more cooperation and respect.

- Lesson: Successful people have found a motivating desire to succeed and nothing will stop them.

People usually want to succeed because they want to meet a motivating desire. My desire has always been to prove to myself that I could accomplish greater goals. It started because I had done poorly as a student in school. I could not compete for the better grades in school, but I learned that I could compete as an adult. In fact, I think it can be said that I've been more successful than most of my former classmates at accomplishing goals in life.

The desire to accomplish does not mean you have to succeed in a do-or-die attitude. Blind ambition and drive simply is the fuel that runs your internal engine that keeps you moving towards your goals of success.

As the story goes on, I went back into my own auto reselling business and I had the opportunity to buy my own property on Sunrise Highway on Long Island. Nothing was going to stop me from getting that property. I had a burning desire to conduct my own business at that location. This time I was smart enough to know I had to own the property. I did not want to worry that some town representative would come by and give me thirty days to leave! I even remembered to get the required town permits this time. I remembered that lesson!

Once I had my Northeast Liquidators business up and running, I was able to go to the auto auctions feeling confident. Over the years, I had built up relationships at the auction houses. I bought so many cars at the auctions I developed my own type of credit that I called "trade credit." Nobody at the auctions had heard of it. I just made it up. Most of the other bidders would not qualify for "trade credit," but the auction houses gave me trade credit because I was such a big buyer. And my checks never bounced!

I now had the financial capacity and clout to bid on almost every car.

There were times when I would bring a car back to my business and have it sold before my check for the car came to my bank a few days later. I sold between 20 to 25 cars a week. One week I bought 62 cars and by the next week we had sold 45 of those cars!

Unlike the regular auto dealers, I did not have cars sitting on my property very long. I had changed careers from being an auto body tradesman to running a successful business. I could have talked myself out of trying in life with the excuse that I was never a good student or some other excuse. But I'm glad I did not let the negatives in my life stop me from trying. After all, I was having fun by now and becoming financially successful.

Risk. Adventure. Blind Ambition. Drive. Success. These are some of the attributes you will need to be successful in life or business.

I like telling people it's always easier to make your first million. The reason is you're willing to take the risks to get started. I am a little more cautious with risks at this point. There were risks that I had taken to get started that I would not take today. For example, I had the pressure of buying $60,000 worth of cars every week, even when I only had $30,000 left in my checking account. I went ahead because I knew I would have them sold by Friday. There are times you will be involved with calculated risks. Sometimes, I would buy a car for $10,000, knowing that I could sell it the next day. The profit on that car would replenish my bank account.

I do not recommend running your bank account down to three dollars. I know the tremendous pressure of running a bank account low, but my blind ambition helped me go out to find the cars that I needed and resell them immediately. I was not about to end my business because of a few cars. That blind ambition kept my business running. After the first years of profits, I had a comfortable money cushion in the bank.

Besides my going to the auctions and buying the cars, I had the logistical problems of having drivers haul x-number of cars from the auction to my Long Island location. I was hauling in so many cars; people would say to me, "Les, you should have your own trucks." I had drivers who would drive three hundred miles to put the cars on a tow truck or trailer and drive them back. I was doing so much hauling the car haulers would almost bid for my work. I let others do the hauling and I kept focused on the car business.

Remember that I wanted my business to be running at 110%. That meant I had to outsmart and do things better than my competition (the other buyers and resellers).

My wife came on board at that time. Now, I know having your wife work with you may not be a good idea for some of you! It worked for me because she shared my same visions. My wife had great experience as a nurse, educator, and administrator, as well as being a great organizer. She started a system that got rid of the liens and helped assign the haulers to each car. Nobody was reclaiming the cars as efficiently as we did. Our paperwork was spotless.

I hired my son. Now, that may not be a good idea for some of you too! He was eighteen and he had taken a course to be a locksmith. Instead of waiting for somebody to find the car keys, which were always lost, I had my son make the keys for the cars before selling them. He also became the youngest buyer in that business.

You do not have to hire your wife, son, or other relatives. The point is you hire those people who will help you reach your 110% production.

I also hired a man to clean the cars and make them more salable.

I subcontracted a tow truck driver to haul 20, 30 or more cars a week.

I was selling cars and other things were happening. I was having fun! I was making money. And I was achieving new heights of success.

Now, remember—I was lucky to get out of school! That's how bad I was in school. Some of you may not have been good in school. I'm here to tell you: being a poor student in school does not always matter. Sure, I know I cannot be a nuclear physicist, but all of us can reach great heights of success. In America, we have the freedom and blessings to become greater than our parents and achieve new heights of success. It doesn't matter if you can't be a physicist or jump high to play basketball but you can still find honest ways to make money and be successful.

What matters is your attitude. What matters is taking an opportunity and finding how you can make life better and turn your life into something successful for you! Other people could not be as successful as I was at my auto reselling. That does not matter. I'm not trying to teach you how to run an auto resell business. I'm showing you examples of how to think differently.

What is it that you are good at? What is it that you

want to work hard at to be successful? Once you know some of these answers, you then need to ask yourself, how can I think in terms of 110%? What 110% efforts do I need to do to be more successful?

When I went out to buy the cars, I had a clear head. I knew my team at the office would help to get each car back to my property where it could be sold. I had about six people working for me which was enough for my business. Joe had seventy people in his business, but he had a yard where about 65 people worked in the auto parts section dismantling the cars and selling the parts. My focus was on bidding, buying, and selling. I was not in the car parts business.

My father had been in the auto collision business. I had learned from his experience and at my body shop that I had once owned. These experiences taught me how to estimate the costs to repair the damage on a car. I knew exactly what that car was worth.

My competition was made up mostly of auto parts men. They knew how many parts the car would need, but they could not figure the labor costs. I had more tools (knowledge) than my competition about the various factors in estimating the worth of a car. I even knew about how color is a factor. I knew the resale value of a red car with a white interior, while knowing that a silver car was usually a lot less.

From the lessons and added experience from working with Joe, I knew what others did not know. I looked at doing business as a game. I knew what to buy and what to reject. When a competitor realized he could not sell a car, he would, sometimes, come to me and offer to sell it to me at half the price he paid just to get rid of it. Occasionally, I would buy a car from a competitor and find a way to resell the car at a profit. I was having fun!

Unfortunately, it was not the kind of business where I could open up other outlets or go nationwide. I had to be realistic. I did not see it as the type of business to expand into a franchise.

For my business, this was the first time that I had all the pieces to the puzzle and the puzzle made sense. As much as the money meant, the accomplishment was just as important!

Another 110% Story At Another Stage of My Life

When I later got into the home inspection business, I found out that not everyone had the drive to work at 110%. Out of 50 people at our home inspection association meeting, there were about 15 people that were doing the same volume of business that I was doing. When I explained to those who were not as successful as me what I was doing to increase my volume of business, I often heard this response, "Oh, I could not work that hard." I never understood thinking that it's such a terrible thing to work hard. Besides, hard work will lead you to working smarter too.

- Lesson: If hard work brings me success *faster*, the time at working hard is worth it.

When I was starting in the home inspection business, I thought, *How can I run my business better? If every business should be doing 110%, what will I do to make that 110% effort in this business?* I had that 110% challenge to meet. Sound familiar? I have to find answers to that 110% effort if I want to be successful.

To do my 110% in the home inspection business, I decided I had to do the following:

- Join the local Kiwanis, Chamber of Commerce, and local groups.

- Visit every real estate office at least three times and drop off my business cards.

- Promote at every opportunity.

- Attend home shows to promote myself.

- Stand on my head! (That's how Robin Williams read the script for the upcoming TV show *Mork and Mindy*, and he got the part!)

- Make those who can give you referrals part of "your team." As an example, my team had to be real estate brokers, real estate attorneys, bankers, contractors, and mortgage lenders.

I used to laugh because the real estate brokers and attorneys must have been thinking that I was running for mayor when they saw me coming by so much. But my efforts separated me from my competition. My competitors might come to a real estate office once and never come back. I kept going back and back and back. Call it hard or easy work, but I believed in expending the effort.

I needed to get the real estate people to be on "my referral team." If they were part of my team, they would feel comfortable to call me. A home inspection is a very unique profession. You get business from the people who want you to reassure the buyer that the home is okay, but your alliance is with the buyer to make sure the buyer knows what he is getting. It's a position that puts the inspector on the fence every day.

- Lesson: Success comes by constantly thinking and finding new ways to grow your business.

In making my contacts in the home inspection business, I came in contact with mortgage bankers. I ended up working with a lot of mortgage companies because they became part of "my referral team." They started giving out my name all the time to refer people to my home inspection business.

About ten years ago, I met Scott, a very driven man and now the president of a successful mortgage company. He now has about 90 people working for him. He seems low key when you talk to him, but I have learned how he is constantly thinking about growing his business. His mind never stops when it comes to business. He never ceases to amaze me. He has been at the 110% level of thinking by involving himself in the following:

- Networking computers in real estate offices to help applicants talk with their loan officers

- A newsletter and newspaper

- He gave a Christmas party where there must have been 250 people. It may have cost him $100,000, but he promotes a business spirit from the party, besides showing his appreciation to his employees.

- A cable television show

- A radio talk show

He invented marketing approaches to promote his mortgage business and that is why he is successful. This is why in 12 years he now has 90 people working for him.

Success Is Not For Everybody

I remember how I used to think everybody wanted to work hard and become successful, just as I did. I've learned not everybody wants to make a lot of money or do the work that it takes to be successful. Again, everybody wants something better in life, but not everybody is willing to apply himself or herself to the 110% effort.

Some people have a fear of success or someone has discouraged the person by telling him or her that they are no good or cannot do anything. I could have thought that about myself as a student. The one thing I never did was to think I was unable to do something great or successful just because I was not a good student. You should not think *anything negative* about yourself! The greater your negative thinking about yourself the less likely you will succeed. On the other hand, we are not encouraging people to become divas who only boast and do not know what they are saying or doing.

It does not take a lot to discourage some people. Some people have a low tolerance for rejection, ridicule, or failure. Failure need not be a bad experience because you will learn something by failing. At that moment of failure, you will be making two choices. You will either remain a failure or you will turn that failure into a steppingstone to success. You can see that most people trip over failure and are unwilling to get up. Make the failure a steppingstone, so you don't lie there and never get up.

It has been said that it took Thomas Edison 1,000 experiments to make a light bulb work. If he had given up on the 999th experiment, we might still be without a light bulb. How many of us would be willing to keep doing the hard work to find a successful light bulb? If we cannot accept rejection, ridicule, and failure, we will never be successful.

- Lesson: Failure, ridicule, and rejection are often helpful at making us realize what we need to do to be successful.

Don't just have what I call a "lottery mentality." That's when you tell yourself, "I'll get rich when I win the lottery." Most people would take the $1,000,000.00, if given to them or they win it in a lottery. If you are willing to take the million dollars, it shows that the idea of having that amount of money is not holding you back. But you have to confront yourself. Are you willing to do the *hard work* and take the *risks* to make a million dollars? I believe you will be able to become a millionaire or be successful, as you define success, only when you change your thinking and find ways to do greater things.

A friend of mine owned a dry cleaning store. In his spare time, he was doing some charity work in a section of town where the people did not have much money. He needed help in his business; He was willing to pay $10 an hour. He asked some of the people who needed the job and the money to come to work for him. He was amazed at the excuses they gave him for not working: "I would need a babysitter"; "I can't get there"; I can only work Mondays and Tuesdays."

What salary would it take to get those same people to come to work for him? $20, $30, $40 an hour? We all want to make the top salary or income, but there are certain people who will not work until they are given an impossible salary. This is no ambition!

There are success stories of people who have started at a low salary and worked under miserable conditions, while gradually positioning themselves to get to the next level.

Without the right attitudes and the fire to make something happen in your life, nothing will happen. Why rely on somebody else making you successful? Why wait for the lottery, which may never come? If you can do something to improve your life, why not start today thinking and doing the 110% to improve your life?

What Are Your New Options Today?

You have to keep looking at your new options. Just as there is a new sunrise every day, you will find a new day can bring a whole new set of options. Maybe you had a new inspiration that will take you to a new level. There is always something new happening. Can you see something new today that could be special for you? You have to always, always be looking for something new coming your way.

Donald Trump started off ahead of the game with the Trump name that his father had established in New York City. Of course, Donald still had to learn how to run the real estate business. But, he used the Trump name to have access to the railroad property, which helped him become successful, even though he never bought it. He used the property hype as leverage to make other people start to think he was a real estate mogul who could give them all the deals. Then he just kept on making more deals.

Henry Ford is someone who started at zero and made

lots of cars. His idea for an assembly line worked successfully and has been copied around the world. It's always a thrill and an inspiration to see how people started out with nothing and made their ideas into a success. The list of millionaires and billionaires is an example of people with nothing and achieving at the 110% level.

Success does not have to be measured by money since success can be measured any way you want.

- Lesson: Successful people stay focused. Other people let the little things get in their way.

With *blind ambition*, you are not going to let anything stop you from your goals and you have no time for excuses.

Chapter 3

Do Your Homework

Whatever you plan to do in life, success cannot be accomplished without knowledge.

Though knowledge is intangible, it can be worth more than all the tangibles you can ever have.

If I want to get into a business or start a business, I know I have to learn everything I can about that business.

- I'll go to the industry's conventions.

- I'll connect with networking clubs.

- I'll go to hear speakers and find speakers' bureaus regarding that industry.

- I'll do internet research about the industry.

- Once I've gone to the seminars and thought about what I've learned, I'll go back to the seminars again.

There are several important reasons for going back to the seminars:

- You will never catch all the ideas at one time.

- You will have more questions that need answering after you have reflected on your new knowledge. You should go back with a list of questions that you would like answered.

- Seminars change, which means there will always be some new information given by the speakers and that will be discussed as a result of your questions or someone else's questions.

When you reach the point where you're ready to reveal to others your new adventure, you should expect to get mixed reviews from your friends and associates.

There will always be the negative comments: "You cannot do that" or "That's a ridiculous idea." Others' statements will be positive, "You're doing great" or "You should be very successful."

You cannot base all your decisions on listening to someone else's comments, whether negative or positive. If someone says to you, "You should be very successful," are they telling you that as a sincere belief in you or do they only want your investment money?

Some people have the habit of being negative because they're afraid to encourage you to do something new. These people find it easier to discourage than to encourage.

It comes down to believing in yourself. You have to maintain a realistic perspective as to how you are doing.

- Lesson: There are always negative (people and experiences) to be encountered in reaching your goals successfully.

The majority of us never have an easy path to success. How many of you have people lay down a red carpet in front you to walk down? If we happen to be a celebrity, we may be given the red carpet treatment. However, celebrities are always in danger of slipping off the success path and losing their popularity, so they have to work at being popular.

Most of the times we earn our success by hard work and outsmarting our competition.

One thing you want to do is to learn what negatives you are about to face in that goal, business, or profession that you seek to make as the path to your success. Remember: there will always be negatives to be encountered, unless you have people giving you the red carpet treatment all the time.

The Pizza Shop Example

For example, say you want to open a pizza shop. You have in your head that a pizza shop is your dream and it's going to make you a millionaire or at least provide you with a comfortable retirement.

You need to stop and say to yourself, "Let me see what I can find out about the pizza business."

- You should begin by interviewing those in the business.

- Talk to at least 10 people in the business. One pizza owner might say, "I work eighty hours a week and I can't get good employees." Another pizza owner might say, "I'm making less than a truck driver who's making $70,000 year, but I'm happy."

- You should talk to as many people who are successful in the business. Ask them what they are doing right. Can you match what they are doing?

- Make your list of the positives and the negatives.

- Analyze your strengths and weakness in handling these different positives and negatives.

Can you handle or overcome the negatives that you found out in your interviews?

You are going to be encountering these negatives. Will the negatives defeat you or will you defeat the negatives?

In your analysis about the pizza shop, you might have seen that the less successful pizza shops do not deliver. If you need to deliver, can you afford to do this? Can you find enough drivers? Can the drivers make enough money to stay?

I went to a seminar a few years ago about shopping center development and management. I learned a lot about shopping centers that I did not know. I could have complained about paying a $600 for the seminar, but the truth is I came back with $10,000,000 worth of knowledge. That knowledge protected me from experiencing a lot of negatives, which could have hurt me if I had not done my homework by attending that seminar.

When a friend of mine wanted to go to the seminar, I said, "I'll go again. I'll go with you."

I heard the same speaker for a second time. I think I learned more the second time because the speaker handled the same material in a different way and I had a better list of questions I was ready to ask.

- Lesson: In business, you may have to collect knowledge that you might not have learned in school in order to become successful.

It is obvious that we will continue to learn as we experience lessons throughout life. Once you graduate from school, you will begin to experience endless opportunities to be successful. All the new knowledge that you learn will become your keys to success. Stay alert. Learn anything that keeps you focused on your path to success.

The first step is getting the knowledge. The second step is up to you to use the knowledge in unique ways to outsmart the competition and to accomplish your goals.

Getting the knowledge means using every source available: You will want to collect this knowledge by attending seminars, taking quick-start courses, networking, interviewing people in your chosen field, and any other way you can learn what you need to learn.

For example, you should not open a pizza shop only to find yourself facing one hundred different problems that you never realized would happen. You want to minimize or eliminate telling yourself, "I didn't know about that."

Running a successful business is an exciting adventure.

The adventure requires that you have both eyes open and be imaginative to dream up those 110% ways to make your adventure work.

- Lesson: Your goal is to reduce the amount of negative issues and problems that may happen to you.

I have friends who are doctors. They have told me that the medical profession has changed for the worse and it is harder to make a living as a doctor. Some doctors have gone into other professions because of too many problems and the cost of running a medical office. Their malpractice insurance may cost anywhere from $50,000 to $500,000 a year. If they have one or more frivolous lawsuits, they may have to pay exorbitant fees for malpractice insurance. Doctors also face problems that come with working for twenty-two insurance companies who want to pay them only on the volume of patients seen, not on the quality of service provided. A good example was owning my own pizza shop.

When I was in the process of building a shopping center, people were coming to me to ask about renting space in my shopping strip center. They were selling me on the idea of renting space to them so they could open a pizza shop. The space is on Sunrise Highway and there are sixty-six thousand cars going by every day. Some were saying, "There's a school in the back, so those kids would be customers too."

I was excited about a pizza shop. A fourth person came in who wanted to open a pizza shop and was willing to give me $10,000 as key money on top of the lease. That's how much he wanted to rent that location.

Naturally, I thought, *If there's that much money in a pizza shop, I guess I'll open my own pizza shop.*

I began by following the first step of my own advice: getting the information and knowledge, in other words, doing my homework.

I researched pizza restaurants. I thought I knew every last detail about the pizza business.

Although I did not know how to make a pizza, I got my son and his friend, Peter, who knew the business, to open up my pizza shop. Peter had already worked in the trade for 5 years and was knowledgeable.

Every business needs a little hook to attract the crowds. I dreamed up the idea of a white stretch limousine out front to deliver the pizzas. To this day, I can tell someone I owned a pizza place along Sunrise Highway and people will ask me, "Was that the one with limo?" The limo may have conjured up images of the godfather running our pizza business, but the white limo made people remember where we were. The limo turned out to be a great hook as a marketing tool! It was a lot of fun too!

- Lesson: Have unique marketing ideas. What do people want to see and what can you do to help people remember you or your business? Have fun marketing.

My marketing approach helped the pizza shop take off like a rocket.

My son and Peter were great at helping the business get started, but I found out I should have done one more thing to see if I could be successful in the pizza business.

I admit now I did not do all my homework. I missed one thing. After you read this book, I hope my mistake will never happen to you.

Even if you have to volunteer to work, go to work in the business or career field for a day or two. In a couple of days, you may find your answer, whether you hate or like what you are about to do in your path to success.

If you find that this one road to success is too bumpy, you still have time and your investment money to go on to a better road to success. You should never have to be stuck on one road to success, especially if that road is killing you.

If I had worked in a pizza shop, I would have seen what I did not want to get into. All along I was used to working with professionals and trained people. I was not used to working with one group of employees: adolescents.

When I dealt with adults who were motivated to work, I was okay. Adolescent employees, who make up most of the employees in my pizza shop business, had me feeling that I had entered the twilight zone. They were too unpredictable about coming to work, especially on Friday and Saturday nights when they wanted to party with their friends.

After two months of problems with the adolescent employees, I threw up my hands and was ready to close the door.

That's when my wife stepped in and said, "Okay, give me the keys. I'll run it." She is a much better manager than me when it comes to employees. I'm more of an idea man. I prefer to be a creator/initiator.

I had the concept of the pizza shop and got the business running successfully. After that, my interest faded because I did not like to micro-manage the place or the people. Once I started marketing, the business started immediately. We were on the local map like McDonald's. We never had to wait for business to build up.

Take the lesson to heart: work in the business or in

what you consider will be your path of success. In a few days, you will begin to see if you really like it and understand what may be the pitfalls/negatives that will challenge you. Meanwhile, my wife ran the pizza shop while I went on to start my next business.

- Lesson: The pitfalls/negatives for someone else may not be a problem for you.

The pizza business was successful because everything else was being done at 110%!

We wound up selling the pizza shop to Peter and Keith, two young men who helped me start the business, and were still working for me. They paid us over five years for the business. One of them still owns the business, after eighteen successful years.

Be honest about what you like and don't like. The sooner in life you decide what you want to do and what you don't want to do the better it is for your success. Do not start a career or a path for success based on what others want you to do. The result is you may only put in an average effort and not the 110% you should be doing. An average student or an average employee cannot expect to succeed. If the food at a restaurant is only average, who wants to go back to that restaurant?

Anybody can be average. The world is made up of a majority of people who are average.

- Lesson: Success requires going beyond being average. Being average is the easy way of life. You can meet your basic needs of food, shelter, and clothing by being average. If you want to achieve real success, you will never accept being average for yourself.

- Lesson: You need a good location and good promotion to be successful.

Most of the time you do need capital to start a business, whether you are trying to start a company like General Motors or candy store.

When you do start on your path to success, there are no guarantees you will make a lot of money from day one. You need to develop a good customer base as soon as possible. Customers are the ones supporting you and your business. You have to make sure customers know you exist and that they have easy access to you.

Those who have found success have stories to tell about the sacrifices they had to make to get started and to become successful. My wife and I remember the lean times when we could not afford a one-week vacation or to go out for dinner. We had to make many sacrifices.

Even movie stars and celebrities remember their struggles and sacrifices before becoming famous.

The lesson is that you should be ready emotionally and financially for the slow times as you get started. You may be lucky to have a lot of customers the first day you open your business. Are you ready to stay open if nobody comes in that first day? Do you know how you can market at the 110% level so you can outsmart your competitor and get more business?

If you are doing your 110% in the right way, the right place, and with the right promotion, you are already on the way to success.

Since I happened to have been in a lot of businesses and professions, I have a lot of people asking for advice. What follows are some ideas for advising people.

If a person has been in a routine job over the years and gets a salary every week, it may be very hard for that person to take on the risk of being an entrepreneur.

I find a lot of people come to me around the age of forty-five. It can be a tough age because you have to look at trying to be successful within a limited number of years, but you can start at any age. By age forty-five, I had already reinvented myself a number of times and had different careers.

- Lesson: Try a franchise if you have no experience because a franchise already has a formula for that business model.

If someone is not experienced in running a business, I like to say, "Go out and buy a franchise."

If you lack business experience, you may well fail. Franchises know fairly well how to operate successfully in various locations. They have gone through the learning curve already and figured things out for you.

New businesses tend to fail in three years or less. That can happen for various reasons:

- not enough long-term working capital.

- not enough customers.

- not in the right location.

- not being a good manager.

- not training the employees properly.

- not having done enough preliminary research.

- being too quickly discouraged by the negatives.

- not working at the 110% effort.

- most importantly, not enough knowledge!

Even if you know how to make a sandwich, what you may not know is how to market your sandwich shop and get enough customers.

Along the way to success, you have to discover whether you are good at managing people. If not, you may need to hire specialists to do certain jobs for you or operate a small business where you only manage yourself.

A Personal Story

A friend of my parents was a corporate middle manager. He and his wife loved to travel to New England and stay in motels on the weekends. When the company she worked for, Mason Candies, a Long Island mint candy company, was sold, he said, "I'm going to buy a small motel." He was given the advice to work in a motel before he used his savings to buy his own small motel. It was a good thing.

When he came back, he had a new awareness that a small motel was not so glamorous. He told everyone, "I can't see how anybody wants to work in this business." On Friday night, he discovered he had to run around to the rooms and change the sheets five times as the prostitutes came and went with their customers. Since he could not afford to buy a Holiday Inn or a Marriott franchise, he learned the pitfalls of running a small motel twenty-four hours a day. He saw where people had broken in to steal the TVs. As soon as he saw the negatives and what could happen to him, he had to find a new path to success.

I was thinking about that story after I opened my pizza shop and I started wondering, *What the heck did I do?* For the same amount of time and effort that it takes to run a small pizza restaurant, I could have invested in a TGI Fridays. I know the financial difference would be better. Instead of making $ 50,000 a year net profits from pizzas, I could be making $500,000 a year net profits in a TGI Fridays. With the better restaurant, I could sell liquor, which is a good way to make more money.

A small pizza shop may be grossing $500,000 a year, but the expenses may be $300,000 or more. In contrast, a TGI Fridays could gross about three million a year. If you made ten percent for yourself, you would still have to worry about the employees coming to work, stealing, and other negatives, but you would be making more money for working the same number of hours in a day.

A small business can always grow, but, if you do not know how to make it grow, you might as well be part of a franchise and cash in on the marketing savvy that comes with that franchise.

It's common sense advice to say, "Look before we leap."

Before you jump into a pool, you want to make sure the water is deep enough. If you want to dive into a pool without knowing all the facts about the pool and the depth of the water, the risks are greater. You could break your neck or die if the water is not deep enough.

- Lesson: Sometimes, you have to change your plans along your path to success as situations change.

When I had gone back into my own auto reselling business, which I called Northeast Liquidator, I sold 22,000 cars in an eight-year period.

After eight years, the auto reselling business was changing and becoming harder to make money.

When I decided it was the best time to closeout Northeast Liquidators, I started developing plans for the property that I owned.

I had come to my next leg of my life's adventure.

I thought I was going to be a shopping center developer!

It took me a couple of years to get the shopping center plans through, but I finally got them approved.

With my own funds, I built a shopping strip center on Sunrise Highway, which is a major thoroughfare.

I became my own general contractor for the building project. Since I did not have all the tenants immediately, I put up the shell of the building and left everything open on the inside.

The extra step that I took was to get a real estate broker's license.

Having the broker's license, I then went to work for the Breslin Realty Development Corp., a leading shopping center brokerage firm. While there, I brought in leasing deals with Nynex, Maaco Auto Painting, and other companies for their properties.

At the same time, I began securing tenants for my shopping center. I had gotten my building rented at exactly the right time. Six months later, I could not have rented the space because the market was starting to fall off.

With the right timing, I had grade-A tenants in my shopping center, such as Aid Auto stores, Subway and Enterprise rent a car. My having taken the extra steps to obtain my brokers license helped me to secure the best tenants.

As a entrepreneur, I have always preferred working on most of my adventures alone. You have to decide whether you prefer to work alone at your success or whether you need a whole team of people helping you or investing in you.

I found I wanted to be a shopping center developer when I realized I could make more money developing commercial space rather than residential. I thought, *Why settle on just building a house and making fifty thousand? I could build shopping centers and make $ 500,000 or $ 5 million.*

The more I learned about commercial development, the more I realized that the land was the key. To own the land, I had to pay big money. I paid $135,000 for the land and living in a house that was worth $60,000. In today's figures, that might be like living in a $800,000 house and paying a 1.5 million for a piece of commercial property. At the time, it was a stretch for me to buy my own land when I did but, I did it anyway.

When the whole economy faltered and money became too tight, I knew I was facing too many negatives. I had to give up the idea of becoming a shopping center developer at that time. After doing more homework, I realized it was not the right time to be on this path.

- Lesson: To be on your way to success, you have to start first by doing your homework.

- Lesson: Take the time to research your idea.

- Lesson: Ask a lot of questions and find out a lot of information.

Chapter 4

Every Door Opens Another Door

The Minivan Adventure

After I did develop my shopping center, I decided to go back to my car dealer roots! People who knew my background in the car business started asking, "Les, do you have any minivans? Can you get me one?"

"Sure, I can get you one." I would say. It was easy for me to go to the auctions and buy minivans for resale.

After a couple of trips to the auto auction, the light bulbs went on.

Light bulb # 1: I looked around and thought, *I don't see other dealers with a lot full of minivans.*

Light bulb # 2: Out of all the people I sold cars to, they all specialized, especially those who were successful. One auto reseller bought and sold Cadillac's. One man was called "Toyota John" because he bought and sold so many

Toyotas. I found that the people who specialized in the same vehicle became experts in those vehicles and knew exactly what to pay for the vehicle.

I found that the Chevy Astro van was not that popular as a minivan, but that it was durable. That's when I decided that I would try selling some minivans. I had a lot in the back of my shopping center that I had built, so I used that space to park the minivans.

- MARKETING STRATEGY: As a marketing tool, I always had a lead item. For this minivan business, I had an customized Astro van in the front of the shopping center.

The business grew to where I was selling about 30 minivans a month and specializing in Astro vans—nothing else! I sold Astro vans with seats, without seats, cargo vans, and anything else the customer wanted. I went back to the auto auctions buying only minivans.

Business had become so good that I had a list of people who wanted certain types of vans. I had such a reputation that the Chevy dealers would send customers to me.

It seemed that, if you get 30 of a specific car, you get labeled as a "specialist."

The 110% Rule paid off: In the first year, I sold over 360 minivans, setting an Astro van record!

- MARKETING STRATEGY: I had a small ad in one paper that read, "Astro vans from $3995. with 25-30 to choose from."

People anxious to get a minivan would call on the phone to ask, "Are you kidding me? Is that ad for real?"

"No, no, I have 25," I would reassure them.

"That many?" the potential customer would ask.

Once a customer knows what he wants to buy, he usually wants to buy that specific vehicle.

Cherry Lane Motors on Long Island used to specialize in selling only station wagons. Other dealerships specialize in Cadillac's and others specialize in trucks.

I found out I could do quite well by specializing. I had a list of what people wanted—white vans, blue ones, and so on. Once I knew what people wanted, I would call the auction house. If they had one, I would come by the next day, buy it, and take it away.

When I got the vans to my place, I got them cleaned at a shop. To service them, I had mechanics at a local shop work on them because I did not want the employee expenses overhead of running my own shop. I subcontracted another mechanic who specialized in checking and repairing the brakes. My overhead expenses were kept to a minimum: an office and a lot full of minivans.

I ended up meeting customers who had been driving all around the Tri-state area looking for the type of van they wanted. Once they saw what I could do for them, they felt it made no sense to waste their time and energy shopping around looking for a van, so we made the sale.

When we sold a van, it was all cash, no financing.

- REMEMBER: I was a "specialist," so I could ask for top dollar and I got it. THE LESSON: Try to be an "expert" in your field.

If a person wants to sell 32 different kinds of toothpicks, that person would be the toothpick specialist and considered an "expert." All that person has to do is make sure he can make money in his business.

- LESSON: Success can lead to competition because people want to imitate your success.

At the auto auction, people were watching me and wondering, "Why is he buying all the Astro vans? He must be making a lot of money somehow with those vans." As soon as somebody thought I must be making money, I began getting competition at the auctions. After a while, I would send my son there and tell him which car to bid on, hoping that no one would recognize him. When my competitors started recognizing my son, I would take my son's friend and tell him which cars to bid on. I was playing the game, which meant I was getting the cars for a better price.

The Van Rental Adventure

P.S. The light bulb went on again.

The light bulb: People started asking me, "Could I rent a van from you?"

The customers had a need. I looked around at the thirty vans in the vans in the back of the shopping center. I saw I could meet their need and make money.

I started to ask the customer. "How much do you want to rent a van for?"

"I'll pay fifteen hundred a week," the customer would say.

"Fifteen hundred a week to rent that van?" I responded, smiling. I thought, I'm only making fifteen hundred selling the van. The rental sounded like a better deal to me.

I looked into the possibility of opening a van rental business, but I found out it is very, very difficult to get auto insurance for this business in New York.

If someone rented a minivan from Avis or Hertz, it might cost $700.

I soon found out that minivans were more often rented in the summer season. People started renting them for fifteen hundred so they could drive to their vacation destinations, such as Disney World in Florida. During my research, I found out that Fantastic Vans on Long Island were always sold out of vans every holiday.

I thought, *I could buy a van for $10,000 and get the $10,000 back with the rentals. With 20 or 30 vans on the lot, this might be a good opportunity.*

I could have rented each van five or six times a year. As good as the idea sounded, I did not pursue establishing the van rental business. At this point, I decided to go back into a former business, auto salvage at a new location.

Starting A Niche Business

In 1992, I went back into the business of reselling damaged cars that could be repaired. The market had changed and if anybody should have known it should have been me. The logistics' of the auto salvage business made it more difficult to process and sell salvage vehicles for a profit. The bad timing left me with some debts. Granted, I still had the shopping center, my house, and some other properties. I certainly did not want to sell off any of my real estate adventures and investments. I needed to follow my own advice in this book, but I had not written down these ideas at that time. The bottom line: I should have done more homework before I went back into my old auto reselling business because the market had changed and was no longer lucrative.

My financial situation had become acute. I decided on starting a business selling tires while I was $250,000 in the hole! I could have very easily put the key in the office door at that point, locked up the shop, and walked away. But, no, that's not me. I wanted to work myself out of the debt. I'm one who wants to think strategically: how do I get out of the $250,000 hole?

I thought, *I'm going to dig myself out of debt somehow. I'm smarter than this predicament. I'll figure it out. How can I make the 110% effort in the tire business? How can I get an angle? How can I get a niche in the tire business just as I had done in my other successful business?*

I wound up going into the tire business in Brooklyn selling new and used low profile tires. Too many businesses sold new tires, so I found the niche in used tires. There was not a lot of competition. I thought, *If I could find used tires and put them all in one place, I would be the king of low profile used tires.* That was between 1992-1995.

- Lesson: Do your homework in order to find your niche.

I started my homework by attending a convention called SEMA (Specialty Equipment Marketing Association). It was for business' that specialized in tires and rims. I talked to the people in the tire business. I investigated the whole tire industry to look for my niche.

By now, I wanted to get out of Brooklyn, so I rented a storefront across the street from my shopping center only because I had no retail space available in my own shopping center.

I felt there seemed to be two basic types of tire business. One business type offered customers a front-end alignment and other services. A person might take his car in for the free alignment and the sales person winds up selling the customer $1,000 worth of tires and services. Some of those services the customer might need, but probably half of the services were not needed. I did not particularly like that end of the business when someone has to "oversell the customer for services not needed," even though it was very lucrative in some stores.

I kept working the tire business six days a week and got it to the point where the business was making a good profit. I was selling tires and at the same time bringing in specialty equipment to sell to the customers. I found myself working with the customers who liked all the fancy car accessories. I called the accessories "jewels," and that term helped to sell more of the accessories.

I carved out a niche in the specialty business. My young customers were coming in to buy rims, which were worth $2,500 with tires. But some of the customers only had $1,800.

I found a solution: I would sell the rims worth $1,500 and gave up trying to sell the younger customers another $1,000 worth of tires. I found out where I could buy the low profile tires cheaper. It turned out to be in Germany! The Germans have a safety rule that the 16, 17, and 18-inch tires on their cars are thrown out if they are worn down more than ¼ inch.

I bought enough of these tires to fill containers that would be brought over to the United States on ships. If I bought one container, I, sometimes, would not get enough of the same tires to make matched sets, but with enough containers we made matched tires sets. I did not know of anybody else on the planet who was ordering tires this way.

I was buying quality German tires for $6 to $8 a piece or about $32 for four tires and then I would match them with my $1,600 worth of rims. For the rims, I was already making a $300-$400 profit and I would sell the $32 worth of tires for another $300 or more.

My niche worked. I was beating my competitors' prices and still making a good $700-$800 on each set of rims and tires, plus selling a lot of other "jewels." By selling two to four sets of rims and tires every day, I was making a profit.

- Lesson: In business, I preferred thinking of putting myself in a "niche market" and that type of thinking is what separated me from my competition.

After four years in the tire business, I had some extra time to do real estate consulting and learn the home inspection business.

The day came when I finally sold the tire business.

Remember: I had brought the business from being $250,000 in the red and the niche provided the breakthrough so I could sell the business for more than $250,000. The tire business gave me the flexible time to step out of the store and keep involved in buying and selling houses and land, which prepared me for my next adventure.

A New Niche: House Inspections

P.S. The light bulb went on again.

Light bulb: As I got back into the real estate business, people were asking me to look at their properties. Meeting this need gave me the incentive to go in another career direction.

I realized I could inspect three or four houses in a day and make a nice fee without a lot of work or financial risk. My previous experience in construction provided me with the knowledge and skills to be a very qualified and professional home inspector. This new field of work also had the potential to open up new doors and new opportunities.

The tire business that I had run successfully and sold continues successfully in business. The pizza business that I sold is still at the same location and operating successfully.

After I sold the tire business, I did not know what the future was going to hold, but I liked the challenge of that uncertainly and set out to make something new happen.

I started branching out into home inspection. Years ago, I had taken architectural design and drafting courses. I had a background in home construction and in developing all phases of real estate. Also, I had the experience of selling houses after I had obtained my real estate broker's license.

I started getting encouragement from people telling

me, "You know houses, so you could do very well as a home inspector." I did not have to be hit over the head a few times to start thinking seriously that there could be a good opportunity in house inspections.

- Lesson: Do your homework thoroughly and you can teach yourself how to be successful.

I started out taking some more courses about home construction. I went to conventions about the housing industry. I learned everything I could about how to do home inspections. In other words, I immersed myself in the home inspection industry.

I began doing a few inspections each week, but I knew I could not make a living doing only a few inspections. I would need to do 10 to 20 home inspections a week in order to take this new career to the next level. In my research, I had found a few successful house inspectors doing that many inspections per week.

I spent time speaking with the successful inspectors in order to discover what made them successful. They shared some tips about being successful. Most of them said it took them ten years to reach their current level of success.

- Lesson: Use the advice of those who are successful to shorten your learning curve.

I had advice from ten successful inspectors who had given me one or more tips. It was up to me to do ten or more things at once and shorten my success curve down to a year.

THE CHALLENGE: how do I outperform the successful house inspectors? I thought, *these inspectors may be book smarter than me. They may even be able to take a test faster than me (thinking back to my school days). But, they do not have my business background about how to expand a business.*

The successful inspectors had their little tricks as to how to be successful, but their success seemed to be taking too long. That's when I decided to start a self-promotion campaign about my home inspection services. I planned on promoting myself aggressively as if I were running for president of the United States.

- Lesson: To be successful, you have to accept the pressures that may come with the occupation.

I'm used to pressure. I'm the one who used to go out and buy $70,000 worth of cars a week and sell them four days later. My competitors never came close to the kind of risk that I had taken. As for most of the home inspectors, they only made up business cards to give to a couple of Realtors. I called that way of marketing "a limited mentality."

I went into the home inspection business with *blind ambition*. It's never good enough just to make a living, as far as I am concerned. I want more out of life. If I had to, I could live frugally, but that's not what challenges me. I told myself, *I'm going to do this. I can achieve becoming number one!*

- Lesson: Develop marketing strategies for yourself that will make you number one in your field.

Every time I had a chance to speak, I would speak about home inspections and real estate, and hand out my business cards.

I looked to hand out business cards everywhere possible—real estate offices, home shows, and real estate shows and conventions.

I became a member of Kiwanis to expand my networking.

I joined the American Society of Home Inspectors (ASHI).

I spent $500 on a booth at a real estate home show.

- Lesson: If you don't *roll the dice*, you're not in the game. The game can be anything you make it.

The booth that I had at real estate and home shows always led to a couple of home inspections, and those inspections led to a couple more referrals. Incidentally at one of the ASHI conventions, my son and I won a brand new Volkswagen because our name got picked out of a hat. You can call it luck, but you've got to be out there at the conventions and in the game in order to have a chance to win.

At the end of the year of constant self-promoting, I went from doing one house inspection a week to doing ten. I had begun outperforming the other home inspectors.

In the local ASHI group of about 60 members, there are only about 20 people working as inspectors and I'm one of the busiest inspectors. The home inspection business does require a good "bedside manner," meaning you have to be friendly, patient, and be willing to explain the good and the bad things that you find with a house. Also, you will get referrals because people will trust your analysis of a house. Still, I believe the home inspection business is one of the hardest businesses in the world to build into a thriving business but, with perseverance, it's all possible.

In the home inspection business, no one will become a multi-millionaire like the developer Donald Trump. However, a successful home inspector can bring in what amounts to double or triple the income some people make in one job, and still have free time.

Another Lesson About The
Mortgage Company

This chapter says every door opens another door. What doors did I find opening for me? First, I started buying and selling real estate at the same time that I worked these other businesses.

I wanted to get a rehab loan when I happened to see a big ad in a newspaper from a mortgage company that struck my attention. I called and talked to a man named Scott for about an hour-and-half.

"When you get a chance, come by with all the information and see me," he said.

When I had my information ready, I drove to his office.

"Do you have an appointment with Scott?" the receptionist asked me.

"Yes, I'm supposed to meet him at 1:30," I said.

As she checked for Scott, I glanced around and saw a lot of people working there. I looked around the front desk and saw only his business card out front. I wondered why only his card was at the receptionist's desk. I picked up the card and saw it identifies him as president of the mortgage company.

When Scott came out, he appeared to be in his late thirties. After introducing himself, he said, "Let me show you around." He certainly had an impressive mortgage business.

During our conversation, we talked about mortgages, home inspections, the weather, the wife, and the kids. He made it seem like he had nothing else to do, but he owned the business and was certainly a busy man.

MAKE A NOTE OF THIS FOR YOUR BUSINESS: he never interrupted our conversation to take another call. I do not always follow that example, but I was very impressed with the amount of attention he gave me.

Another Door Opens

While waiting for the lawyer to process the paperwork on my rehab loan, I spoke with Scott about engineering reports for my home inspection business.

After we talked a while, Scott's lawyer mentioned his TV show.

"A TV show? But he's into mortgages," I said, surprised. Today, Scott has 10 hours of time on TV and the radio.

The lawyer told me about Scott's two-hour cable TV show on Saturdays and Sundays. He said, "Scott ought to put you on that show. I learned more about home inspection in the half-hour sitting here talking to you than I knew before. Let me have your card."

The lawyer turned into a lead for me and opened another door. I was not out of the closing ten minutes when Scott called me. He said, "Oh, Les, I meant to say when you were here that we have a TV show. We would like to invite you on it to talk about home inspections. You can just go on and it would be good exposure for you in your business and we like to keep our customers informed."

"Fine," I agreed.

Since his call, I have been on his show several times over the period of three years. And I have gotten a leads from the cable TV show and gained credibility!

The mortgage meeting opened a door that led to the TV show where I picked up new leads. If I had to pay for TV advertisement time, it would not be worth it because I do not get enough leads to pay the cost of a TV commercial but for free it's great. Being a consultant on TV is an activity that creates activity. In other words, my unpaid TV consulting generated new business for me every week.

As an added benefit, Scott invited me to his grand Christmas party. I jokingly told Scott, "I consider myself by now part of the woodwork at the mortgage company because I'm working with you so much." That relationship still lasts to this day.

One Door Opens Another Door

During the week of the World Trade Center crisis, I had only one home inspection because people stopped thinking about buying or selling homes, but I still made a decent income because I had established so many other avenues of work. Right after the World Trace Center collapse, I attended a local meeting of the home inspectors. The inspectors who do the work part-time had no work. The full-time inspectors, who usually did ten inspections a week, had a two-thirds drop in their business. All the inspectors were hurting. I remained busy because of all the different types of inspections and related business I had built around my core home inspection business.

My home inspection business led me to open new doors:

- oil tank inspections
- a 203 K loan coordinator inspections required for some businesses by the federal government,
- roof inspections
- expediting building permits.

My son is also in the same business and works as my "backup" when I get busy.

I've found through the years that every door opens up another door. It certainly helps to see those doors of opportunity around you.

- Lesson: Not only do you have to stay alert to see the doors of opportunity around you, but the quality and reputation of your work count in opening another door.

I've been a part-time real estate broker for 30 years. I've known many residential rehab companies, but many of them do not do the right job. One company now rehabs 60 houses a month, making about $50,000-$60,000 a house. They're making millions, but they do not do the job right. There's another company that rehabs about 30 houses a month and makes only $30,000 a house, but it does the work right. I still will rehab a house and flip it, or hold it, if the deal is right.

If I have to make a referral, I lean towards the company that rehabs 30 houses a month because it does the job right. The other people may make a ton of money, but they're in court all the time because of the home owners' complaints and lawsuits.

Most home inspectors work one county. I'm willing to work the five boroughs of Manhattan and the two counties of Long Island.

- Lesson: Do more than your competitors are willing to do.

As my home inspection customers move into new homes in new areas, my business expands because they will likely call me again when they want to sell their homes. I have found home inspections are an excellent word-of-mouth business: one person can refer a lot of other people to you, if they trust you.

If I'm at a Christmas party or an event, I always hand out my business cards.

- Lesson: Self-promotion and networking brings in results. You need to expand your networking contacts in order to excel beyond your competition.

A home inspection usually takes me 1.5 hours, plus 20 minutes to write the report, and another 10 minutes to go over the report with the customers. Of course, if it's a large house, I have to charge more money because the inspection takes more time.

The first question people ask me is: "How much do you charge?"

I then have to ask intelligent and fair questions in order to come up with a fair price. My primary question is: "What town is the house in?" If they tell me Levittown, I know by the location that I'll be inspecting a normal size house.

If someone tells me it's Muttontown, an exclusive area, I then go to my next defining question: "How many bathrooms do you have?" If they say eleven, I know the inspection is going to take longer and the fee will be higher.

- Lesson: Show that you can be fair with prices. In order to come up with a fair price, you have to ask intelligent questions and price it accordingly.

To recapitulate, I bought, built and sold a number of houses and I bought and sold a lot of land. I became involved in real estate and real estate related businesses over the years.

- I had to be in the game to find a new door of opportunity.

- I was learning all the time—about a niche and about new doors that were always there.

- When I saw a door of opportunity, I acted.

- Whether you act a day early or a day late, you need to be ready and willing to take action to make something happen.

- Great timing is a good asset.

Chapter 5

Life's An Adventure

When I was young, my parents used to say I was a dreamer. A lot of things I dreamed about came true because I went out, worked hard, and found ways to achieve my dreams. Even as a young boy, I made an adventure out of accomplishing what I wanted to do.

Life is an adventure because I've always looked at the glass in a positive way—as being half full, not half empty.

When you are very poor, you may find it very difficult to be happy most of the time because you are focused too much on making the next dollar, trying to survive, and the slightest difficulty can set you back financially. We would note that money doesn't bring happiness, but your state of mind will. Everybody has a different idea of happiness. Someone who appears to have enough money in the bank and appears financial secure may be considered "happy" on the surface, but that person may have a different set of worries.

I was listening to someone make cold calls on stores to sell them particular items. This caller was very successful. He said, "Even if the owners were not interested in what I'm selling, I will always tell them to have a great day, which I meant sincerely, not sarcastically." He pumped himself up so he could get to that next cold call and be enthused.

I find I operate in business the same way. I want to stay positive. I don't want to bring myself down with the negatives that come along in life.

- Lesson: The more positives you have in your thinking the less likely you will fail. Spend your time thinking how to improve yourself, not in reliving the past or focusing on what goes wrong.

Positive attributes are like vitamins. If you are missing an important vitamin, you are going to feel bad and become sick. If you do not have enough positive thinking, you are going to turn into a mental, emotional, and personal wreck.

Once in a while, I do feel down or upset. I am human. But I try to find something positive that happened during the day, the week, or the month to focus on, instead of focusing on the negatives. One way I keep motivated is to repeat to myself, "Life is an adventure." It is! There are so many fascinating opportunities that come along, so many people we meet who can help us, and so many new doors of opportunity that we can open.

When I was a young man, I would, sometimes, be telling people about some of my accomplishments. I don't think they did believed me. Why? Because by age 25, I had been one of those who had already jumped around in 15 jobs. It sounds ridiculous. But my life had been a roller coaster ride. Those who know me have come to realize that I had changed occupations and career directions, not because I had to, but because I wanted to. I could have stayed with any one of my jobs or professions and have remained reasonably happy, but I became bored after a while and wanted to take advantage of another door of opportunity opening.

Eventually, you have to put in the 110% effort, to find your blind ambition, to do your homework, and to see your new door of opportunity, but the next big step is the one that some people are afraid to take: the plunge—you have to *roll the dice* to be in the game. If you don't try to do something different or better, you can never get to the next level.

Someone gave me a small key chain of a hand with a pair of dice in it. I carry it with me all the time.

"What are you, a dice player or a gambler?" People have asked me when they see it.

No, I'm not a gambler. I may go to Las Vegas and lose

a hundred bucks at a table, but I'm in control of how to play a game. I will not lose ten grand on frivolous gambling. I believe the real adventure is not in gambling, but in finding the doors of opportunities. Life is an adventure, not a game of blackjack.

You can lose money at anything in life. People have lost their retirement investments when they trusted the stock market, the IPOs, or major corporations, such as Enron and WorldCom. We know what happened to those so-called "safe" investments.

One thing you will always have are your adventures and, hopefully, good memories. I'm so stuck on the idea that life is an adventure that I named my latest boat, "Adventure Nine." People ask me, "Why that name?" I say, "It's my ninth powerboat." In fact, I bought and sold powerboats for a while, but this was my ninth personal boat.

Always "Play the Game" Honestly

When I resold damaged cars, I played the role of middleman between the insurance company or dealership cars at the auctions and the body shops. I learned early on that for most every car that was fixed there was some chop shop stealing one and selling the parts. The police auto squad had even investigated my business at one point. The police could not believe that I was involved in dealing with so many people in this auto reselling business and doing it legitimately.

"How do you stay legitimate when a lot of salvage businesses are operating on the edge or illegally?" the police asked me.

"If they are doing something illegal, they will get caught. I'm not interested in that type of business. I'm interested in the game," I said.

That's the word Joe reinforced in me – the game, game, game, game, game.

You can work on the edge and you can push the envelope to perfect the game honestly!

- Lesson: The only worthwhile success, whether is comes as money or goals, is based on honesty.

Sometimes, people feel they have to go to the edge to make money, but you don't have to steal anything. Do you think the people at McDonald's go out and steal hamburger meat and then sells hamburgers to their customers? Stealing is not the way to run a successful business and it's not the way to run your life. McDonald's has a system that works. It is important to find a system that works for you and the business.

- Lesson: You need to find a new system that works better for you, so you can accept the new risks of the game and accomplish the new rewards.

- How many athletes think about tearing their ligaments or breaking a bone when they go into a game? This is risk verses reward.

If they worried about those negative possibilities, which are real, they would not be able to play the game. They certainly could never be champions. In most sports, there are dangers in the game. Even in the "safe" game of golf, Tiger Woods knows well enough that he could be struck by lightning, unless he gets off the course before a storm intensifies. But he would never stop playing golf because lightning might strike. Some people get stuck in the "what ifs" of negative thinking so much that they cannot go out and play the game.

When some people come to me and say, "Les, I want to go into business, what should I do?"

"Have you ever been in business before?" I ask them.

"No," some of them reply.

"Then go buy a franchise," I tell them.

"Why?" That's their response and they ask it looking surprised.

"Because that franchise has worked out the formula,

the formula, the formula," I say emphatically.

From Joe, I learned the concept of "the formula." There's a formula to everything. Everything that I've done since Joe, I have looked for the formulas and tried to make every business into a science.

I stayed on with Joe as long as I did because I was learning so much. What he taught me about doing business and the philosophy about doing business was worth more than gold. What he taught me were ideas and concepts that I could apply in any business or anything I did in life.

I also want to say that there were many other employees who worked for Joe, but I was one of the few, if any, who used his knowledge effectively. You have to learn to apply your new knowledge and not just let it sit aside.

- Lesson: Success often has to be learned – how to play the game, the philosophy and attitudes that win, and the formulas that work the best.

Chapter 6

Be A Good Card Player

I think about the song *The Gambler* by Kenny Rogers and he had a line in there about when to hold and when to fold the cards. A good card player knows when to hold and when to fold. Folding the cards and walking away at the right time can be a strategy for success too. In business and in life, I see too many people hang on to something that's going into a dead end.

I'm not saying it's easy to fold. If you're in business or in life relationships, you may have to analyze all your options before you conclude you have to close the business or end a relationship.

- Lesson: Being in business requires you to analyze how well you are doing and what you can do to improve the business.

Lifeboat Story

I've seen people get into situations where their once successful business seems to be going backwards because, sometimes, outside forces change things and make business obsolete! They only stay in the business because they feel comfortable and are used to what they have. Some people stay on running a business when they are not making a profit. They may be down to the point where they are making nothing. They're showing up everyday, having all the obligations of paying employees, but they are going home with nothing. At that point, it's very easy to get into negative thinking. They have negative thinking usually because they are afraid to change.

I'm not going to tell anyone that it is easy to jump ship. I've seen people get to the point where they are exhausted because they're constantly putting out fires. They're putting out fires to stay afloat and they're exhausted and cannot see where they are going. And if their boat sinks, they go down with it. People get themselves into financial difficulties. That is why there are bankruptcies. I'm not telling anybody to go bankrupt, but a person may have to liquidate the business or liquidate the situation. It may be one of the toughest things you have to do, but you can get off the sinking boat and get into a lifeboat, if you plan ahead.

A lifeboat is not as big as your original business or situation, but you are safe, until you get on with your next opportunity.

You may not be able to afford to keep driving the Rolls Royce you once drove. What is more important is that your mind is clear. You're off the Titanic that was going down. Once your mind is clear, you can start over again and do better. What did not work out can help you do better. That lifeboat can take you to a bigger boat and you can start a whole new adventure.

If someone asks me for advice and I see something going wrong from my perspective, I try to explain the lifeboat story. Years later, I've had many people come back to me and say, "I was thinking about what you said. I came to realize that I had to make a change and get my head clear so I could start on my next journey."

Reflections Can Affect Your Success

You have to keep alert that you do not let a relationship ruin your opportunities.

I've seen people locked in a situation or they think they're locked into a situation, whether financially or emotionally with a partner. You can always close a business or change an occupation. It's harder to change a relationship because the other parties may not cooperate or they want more control than you are willing to give up.

You have to enter business partnerships knowing you may have to take your share of lumps and bumps. Even a marriage has its difficulties too. You may have to get into the lifeboat because the partnership/relationship is taking an emotional toll on your health and attitudes. For example, your associate or partner may not see your vision of what has to done. It can happen that the wrong business partner can slow down the business. People can become stubborn, so you need to know a partner's temperament to see if that person is going to help or hurt the business before you become partners.

Sometimes, the partnership works out, but the business idea does not work out.

Other times, I have experienced a partnership where I felt overburdened because I was doing eighty percent of the work and the partner was not doing the necessary fifty-fifty share of the work or vice versa. You may have to make changes before you get hurt.

I am not suggesting that both partners always have to do the same thing. In the restaurant business, one partner might be doing the cooking. The other partner might be working hard to greet the customers and to promote the business. Both partners are key to a successful business.

When someone comes to me and says, "I want to

improve the business. By the way, I do have a partner."

"What does the partner do?" I ask.

"My partner provides the money," the person may say.

That can be a difficult situation because the person with the money will want a lot of assurances and those assurances may be difficult to meet.

I prefer to tell people, "If there is any way you can start your business without a partner, you may prefer to do that because you will have more control. If you have a good idea and a way to meet the needs of your customers, you should be able to make money without relying on a partner if you can.

- Lesson: Partners work great if each one works a different end of the business and compliment each other . That's when the magic happens.

If you only have fifty percent control, you are counting on the other person to complement the other fifty percent. It's like a car: you want to operate on your four cylinders and you want your partner to operate on his four cylinders. If your partner is not operating with his four cylinders, then you have to start working with more cylinders of your own to take up the slack.

When four cylinders and another four cylinders accomplish the work of twelve cylinders that's called magic. It can also be called synergy. That's when two partners create more than the sum of their individual parts.

- Lesson: Just having a financial business partner may not be the total solution to your business or goals.

I tend to believe that ninety-five out of a hundred financial partnerships usually tend to fail for various reasons. Partnerships can be a tricky business, as we have already hinted at – impatience by one partner for seeing results, lack of sharing an equal amount of work, or different visions of the business goals.

I still suggest to people to look into franchise businesses because the franchises have worked out a formula for that specific niche business. With the franchise, you are using their advertising, marketing, and tools that are already established.

WARNING: YOUR BUSINESS COULD FAIL IN THE FIRST THREE YEARS.

The Small Business Administration (SBA) keeps all the statistics on small business failures. One of the first things you need is to have capitol to carry you through three years. Otherwise, you are statistically destined to fail as soon as you open your business.

Ask yourself, "Do I have the capital to finance myself through a calamity?"

You may have to deal with any or all of these types of calamities that could spin your business out of control:

- Downturns in the market

- Loss of appeal for your product or service

- Recessions

- Inflation

- Wars

- Strikes

- Bad publicity

- Increased taxes

- Bankrupt suppliers

- Location disasters, such as floods, rain damage, or droughts

- Terrorists and security problems

What happened on 9/11 sent calamitous shock waves to businesses from Lower Manhattan to across the country. In some instances, state or federal aid may help a business recover. The best way to recover is to have the capital to survive the bad events and the hard times that hit every economy and every business.

- Choice of locations plays a major role in the determining success.

- In my businesses, I always had only one location. I know many business people who have businesses in more than one location. I have always been a hands-on entrepreneur. Running a business in other locations usually requires hiring the right managers to run the operations.

It was my personal preference not to operate a business with multiple sites or to turn my business into a franchise, but maybe that's coming. Management of a business is not my strong point. I recognize my strong points as formulating the daily concept and vision for a business and promoting it, whether it's donuts, cars, tires, pizzas, trains or real estate. The specific business does not matter because the same principles apply.

If you want to turn your existing business into a franchise, I offer this advice: Get the basics down firmly and prove you have an established market. That can take a couple of years. You can usually expand your business into a franchise if you have at least the following:

- An established marketing appeal to the customers

- An established product that customers want during the good and bad times

- Avoidance of dishonesty

- Adequate financial support for more than one location

- A fair distribution of wealth that creates good morale

- Good relations within the franchise

Another thing that I have seen through the years is too many people roll the dice too quickly, which means they may not have done all the homework or have all the knowledge before they venture into business decisions. On the other hand, many people wait a lifetime to roll the dice, which means they are constantly losing opportunities around them.

I have found that men are more willing to roll the dice, while women like more security in a career or business adventure. We have to realize that everybody has a different comfort level when it comes to "rolling the dice," or taking those personal, career, and business risks.

"How can I give up my job I've had for twenty years?" people have asked me.

I'm not going to be the one to tell them to give up what they have. Security is very important, especially today when people need health insurance as part of their "security package." You may have to list what you want in your "security package" in order to decide whether you can take risks, how long you can endure without that part of your security package, and whether your new success will provide all that you need in your security package. There are a lot of things to take into consideration before you "roll the dice." Once you roll the dice, you may not be able to add anything to your security package until you become successful, which may take five years or more depending on your marketing and your customer response.

I go back to the franchise concept. Someone can be very limited with business savvy but can likely run a successful Subway sandwich shop. Why? Because the bread comes the same way, the formula comes the same way – you put two pieces of cheese on, four pieces of this, that and the other thing, and your rent is X amount. Are you going to get super rich doing it? No. Could you have multiple locations that are successful? Yes. If you have the money, you could have a location in Times Square or at the Los Angeles Airport. I don't sell franchises, but if I wanted to, I believe I would be very successful at it because I do believe in them. It's a great business model.

Personally, I always enjoyed coming up with my own idea, formulating it, and putting it into action, which is probably about as far as you can go in the risk factor.

If a person comes to me and says, "I would really like to have an X business," the first thing I'm going to tell that person is, "Go to work in the place. Even if you're an executive, go in and cut sandwich meat on Saturday, whatever you can do to see what that work is like. Even if you work there for free, get an idea what that work is like. Even if the owner may look at you and think you're crazy, get an idea what that work is like."

- Lesson: Work at the business before you decide to invest in the business.

You have to find out how much of a risk factor there is for putting the business together. If the risk factor is ten to one, that business or career adventure may not be for you. By *doing your homework* and *having determination*, you will likely be able to find a way to make it work.

One thing I always tell people is that *you've got to roll the dice to be in the game.* That does not mean taking the family fortune and putting it into a pizza restaurant or any other career adventure where you have never worked.

I'm not big on the stock market. It's great for some people, but it's not for me. Why? I do not have control over the stock fortunes. Stock investors have to keep their stable stocks at the bottom of the pyramid. Keep your riskier stocks in small amounts at the top of the pyramid.

It's the same thing with trying a new business or a new adventure. You don't want to bet the bank or your inheritance all at once. I will admit I did do that one time early in my career. The business worked out because I had more determination with that added risk to work like ten people put together and I had the knowledge. I was going to be successful. Just so you know, I'm speaking about the auto salvage business called Northeast Liquidators.

For the first two years, there was a new obstacle every day. One thing went backwards every day and three things in the business went forward. It's smart to know there will likely be one thing to go wrong every day. Once I had the other things going right, the business was very profitable. It goes back to my favorite saying: *you have to roll the dice to be in the game.*

If you talk, and talk, and talk about doing something, you may talk yourself out of taking action. If you go ahead with your business or adventure, look for the formula to win and don't bet all your savings. Have financial backing for a number of years. I bet the bank when I was thirty and thirty-five, but I would never recommend doing that. I don't believe in "luck" now because I believe in using a formula and being very determined in accomplishing my goals. Without a formula, you better hope you have luck because that may be all you have, and that's not good odds.

- Lesson: One reason not to bet the bank on your adventure is that you will be learning as you go. If you do not learn fast enough or all you need to know, you may fail.

If you don't feel comfortable about your adventure and feel you do not know enough, then stay where you are, until you are ready.

Your Decisions Are Critical To Your Success

Running a business to me is simple, while relationships are a lot more difficult. You can close the door on a business, but you can't just close the door on relationships and partnerships too easily.

After reading this book, maybe some people will say, "I'm not ready to have my own business." That may be the best thing to happen for them. Honesty is part of how you play the game.

When I was a child going to Sunday school, I remember seeing a short film about someone on his way to heaven after he died. He was walking around on top of the cloud, while carrying his cross. He put his cross down and looked at all the other crosses. Then he picked up his own cross and went back down to earth. After looking around, you may not want to do what it takes to reach your goal. The cross may be too hard to carry. You may think, if that's what it's going to take to get there, I'll just stay where I am. In other words, you may be happy with basic successes in life, buying a new condo, or learning to paint.

If this book has helped you make a decision for your life, it was the best money you ever spent because you're going to be a better person for your decision.

When I used to be in the car business, we used a book called the *Galves Auto Price List,* published in the Bronx and used nationwide. For example, the guide gave everyone a good idea what a two year old Mustang was worth. The directory is only a guide, which means you have to take what is in the guide and see how it relates to you. Every car and every situation is going to relate to everyone differently.

The ideas in this book are a guide for your adventures in life.

- Lesson: An important point in this book is about making decisions and acting on your decisions.

I encourage you to make goals and not money as your priority. Money alone does not create happiness. The first step to happiness is to find goals that you enjoy doing. As you accomplish your new goals, you may discover you may not need to make a million dollar income.

- Lesson: A business, profession, or career should be something that you enjoy, where you wake up in the morning and can't wait to get to work. If you're doing something that you enjoy, it's never going to be just considered "work" in your mind.

On the other hand, I do not encourage someone to be a workaholic. That person may not know how to take time off. There are times a person needs to rest his brain from the business. A rested brain will be better able to see new insights, which are part of creativity, problem-solving, and finding success.

When you are happy, you tend to be focused and directed in such a way that you become more successful. Happiness and success can be the best medicine for your health.   The money will come from your happiness and success.

This book is a way of sharing important ideas that should help you. I look forward to hearing from all my readers. When I played and sang in a band, I remember the magic connection when the audience clapped in appreciation. The same holds for this book, except this book can be more important than all the music I ever played. This book can improve your life. My music was simply for entertainment. The difference is this book offers ways to improve your life and career. The more this book has made your life better the happier I will be.

Chapter 7

Looking Outside the Box

Christopher Columbus discovered America at a time when many people thought the world was flat. Sometimes, I feel like Christopher Columbus because I've been in a situation and don't know what I will find on the horizon. I wonder, if I venture all the way to the horizon, will my life be better or will I fall off the edge? The fear of the unknown can either drive us forward in the excitement of wanting to find something new or it will become the fear in us that holds us back in order to feel safe.

Keep in mind that Columbus wanted to prove he had a better concept. People who can conceptualize can be the ones who will be successful.

We see on television almost every day the conditions in poor countries. People ask, "How can people live that way?" It seems to us that they are living 600 years behind our way of life. Their way of life is not "modern," not "convenient," not "comfortable," and very "primitive." If you give the primitive people a satellite TV and let them know how the rest of the world is living, they will likely want to start changing their lives and demanding what is modern, convenient, and comfortable too.

- Lesson: When people see (conceptualize) they can have a better life, they become motivated to want a better life.

It is interesting to see that the terrorist and religious radicals of the world who hate western culture still use cell phones and other inventions that were created in the western world where people are encouraged to be free in their thinking.

I want you to see how you can have a better life. This book can be like your satellite TV. You can start to find your way to a better life.

We have all heard the expression "the grass looks greener on the other side of the fence." What did it take to make that grass greener? It may have taken a lot of fertilizer, know how, and hard work to make it greener.

Are you willing to learn all that you can and work hard to make the grass that you have on your side of the fence as green as or greener than what someone else has?

After this book is published, I'll be reading the book again every couple of months, just to keep myself in check. I remember one time being very comfortable, so comfortable that I missed an opportunity right around the corner. After I saw the opportunity that I had missed, I thought, *Wow, it was right there. I should have found out about that.* As an analogy, you might be heading your boat for one port and, along the way, you find out that the other port will be more successful for you.

- Lesson: Thinking outside the box means having the insight to look around for better opportunities and to make adjustments in your directions in life.

If you research ten antique shops, you are looking at ten different lives. One antique shop owner may say, "I'm a compulsive shopper. I drive to Pennsylvania every weekend and this is what we find and bring back. We're not making a lot money, but we're open three days a week." At the next antique shop, the owner says, "I'm an attorney and I do this antique business on the side."

Each store is operated differently. Each store is different as to how neat it is. Each owner has a different set of motivations. Among those ten shop owners, one may think "outside the box" by finding new markets to sell what he has. He may become a supplier to Macy's or Pier 1

Imports or he may sell on eBay on the Internet. That "little store" has the potential for selling to thousands of people across the country or around the world. Meanwhile, the other nine shop owners are mentally wrapped up in their small store—and their comfort zone.

If I saw I was selling twenty-five of something every week, I'm the kind of guy who would be on the phone to the big department stores to set myself up as their exclusive importer or supplier.

In the end, you have to go beyond your comfort zone and expand your contacts.

I'm a person who takes an idea and, instead of seeing all the negatives, I look for what the opportunity has to offer. Of course, you should always list the positive and negatives on a sheet of paper in order to get a better idea of what you see. Then it would be good to have a trusted friend or consultant look over the list to add ideas to either column so you do not miss anything.

If it looks good and I want to make the idea work, I find I go through at least two stages in developing an idea. Stage One is the feeling of euphoria. I may think, *I like the concept.* I may even feel a high. Then I start wondering, *What will I be getting out of this? Is this going to help me? Is this going to work for me? Financially, does it make sense?* I feel the excitement for two or three weeks as I develop the concept.

Stage Two is the work zone. That's when I put the concept of the idea into practice. It may not be easy and, sometimes, it can take a couple of years to bring the idea into reality.

The older we get the more we just want to get into any safe port and be done with looking for the adventures and opportunities. That attitude of safe port can be good, but it can be bad when we fail to open the door of opportunity in front of us.

- Lesson: Everything you do in life requires a good foundation.

When you go into a new business venture, you have to go back to square one. You have to make sure everything is done right and that the foundation is properly laid for that business.

It's like going back to make sure you can ride the bicycle without the training wheels.

Again, work for at least a week in a position in your new venture. Why? You will quickly see if you like your new venture idea. If you don't work as the helper, you may fail to learn how to make the new venture better later on.

Years ago, I was playing in a band with another young man whose father owned a very successful tool and die business. That young man had the idea of starting in the business as the vice president. The day came when his father asked him, "Would you like to come into business with me?" He said, "That would be great. Where's my desk?" He got a little surprise when his father said, "There's the broom. First, you've got to sweep the shop." The young man said, "But I want my own office." The father said, "No. First, learn how to clean the place. See what is happening in the shop around you. What is being thrown away and why? Is money being wasted somewhere? Then I'm going to show you how to be a tool and die maker. You're going to work with the guys on the line. Eventually, you'll become a manager. You can have the keys someday when you prove yourself. But you've got to prove you can look around and see what is happening in the shop."

That was quite a mental blow for this young man, so he left to go down a rocky road of his own for many years. Eighteen years later, he came back to his father, thinking, Maybe my father wasn't too far off. He had learned the business working for someone else, but he went back to work with his father, who now had become sick. The last I heard was that he owns the company and he has been quite successful. As a young man, he thought naively that he was going to go in and take over without knowing what was happening at the bottom of the business.

For anyone who has been successful in another walk of life, I am not going to tell anybody it is easy to go back and pick up that broom. But the experience with the broom does not hurt. If you do not know the business from the bottom up, you may not be able to handle the business from the top down.

As a home inspector, I have inspected homes in a town where those homes lean all the time because the foundations were never put in properly. If a good foundation is so important to the value and safety of a house, consider how much more important it is to have a solid foundation in your knowledge, your homework, and your attitudes before you go into a new venture.

Your next move may be lateral or vertical. It may be up or down. Whatever the case, you have to look outside the box.

I find it hard to comprehend why people get so satisfied with life that they do not do this. I'm the one who spends more time looking outside the box than I do sitting with my feet up watching the box.

Consultants are people paid to look outside the box. A business owner may be filled with negatives because he feels boxed in. The consultant should be able to show that person new opportunities the owner may have missed.

If you ask a doctor, "How is business?" He may complain, "It's terrible. The insurance companies don't pay me." It is true that the medical profession has changed because of the rising cost of malpractice insurance and the rising numbers of malpractice lawsuits. There are doctors who prefer that their own children not become doctors because of the rising costs and problems in the profession. Doctors are being forced to look outside the box. They have to rethink their own profession and location.

In order to achieve more, you have to ask yourself any number of important questions.

- Are you thinking hard enough about changes or improvements you can make in your life?

- Are you thinking about your potential and how to use your potential in new ways?

- Are you doing enough research and talking to enough people to get new ideas?

- Are you thinking out of the box?

To be successful, you usually have to test how far you can go on the edge of the envelope.

You need to go as far you can and see what happens

in what you want to try. You may surprise yourself about what new things you accomplish.

There are some people who are not conceptual thinkers. Those people want a safe life and a steady income without the risks.

What many people need to learn is to look for new *concepts* for their lives. A change in concepts usually brings new success. You have to be a conceptual person to reach greater success.

In counseling people, I have found that some people often do not set their goals high enough. Fear usually precludes the notion that we can not achieve something. It helps to set goals that are realistic so you enjoy the feeling of success and fulfillment.

- Lesson: Its helps to set goals to reach plateaus.

Unrealistically high goals will likely fail. It is better to reach one plateau. That makes you ready for the next plateau, besides giving you confidence and providing the new learning experiences that you need.

Set a new goal for yourself every month or every week! A year from now you will surprise yourself as to how much better off you are and how much knowledge you have gained.

Another stumbling block is that people get too mixed up with their daily chores and lives. Although worries are real, some people worry too much and stagnate. We all have something to worry about. Very few people live without worries. Worrying can keep us looking at the walls of the box and not to new solutions that lie outside the box.

- Lesson: Don't let your emotions get in the way of clear thinking.

I went to a lawyer one day to talk about suing someone.

"Les, why do you want to sue him? To get back at him for some emotional gratification or do you want the money?" he asked.

"I'd like to get both. I'd like to get my cake and eat it too," I said.

"Call me in two weeks. Tell me what you want to do," he said.

The first two weeks I was ticked off, and I wanted the emotional revenge. At the end of the two weeks, I said to the lawyer, "I just want the money."

Instead of going through the time and trouble of an expensive lawsuit, I put a lien on the property. If I sued the man, I may have won, but the legal expense would have eaten up all the money the man owed me.

Eventually, some day, I will get the money. When he goes to sell the property, he will have to settle the lien and cut a check for me. That will drive him out of his mind. In that way, I've won both the money and the emotional satisfaction.

Be careful of emotions that may cloud your *total view.*

Most people who have one business are not thinking hard enough. For example, there are a lot of people who own only one pizza shop. In Manhattan, there is a business called Ray's Pizza. How many pizza places does he have? Forty. He thought a little harder and found ways to expand his business and his opportunities.

McDonald's thought a little harder in order to expand globally. Even in corporations, there is a great need for conceptual people. The conceptual person is the one who thinks a little harder every day in order to make better things happen.

Anyone in America has opportunities to conceptualize. Many opportunities surround us.

- Lesson: People will find it hard to succeed if they do not expand their concepts.

When I have a new idea for a business, I go back to Joe's story about the person who owned a restaurant. When you go there, the valet knows your name. The maître d' knows your name. The waiters and waitresses come by to see if you need anything. Everybody there, not just the owner, is thinking 110% to make your time at the restaurant the most pleasant it could ever be. You go back because you like everything about the place. That restaurant stays in business, while other restaurants go out of business. Giving 110% can be hard for some employees who can't think outside the box. They forget to please the customers and only want to please themselves for the hours they have to be at work.

My wife is an example of someone who is very comfortable sharing my adventures. Yet, she could be in her own business. She managed the pizza business and did well, but she did not conceptualize on the opportunities. If she conceptualized more, she may have gone on to open a franchise of forty pizza shops. Some people are better managers than they are entrepreneurs and that can be all right. The main point is to make sure you look outside the box, which means, do not limit your thinking to just one plateau of life.

After going through this book and considering all the different concepts, you may still want to be a manager. That is okay too. We believe you can take these concepts and make your manager position better.

Some people have come to me and said, "Les, I want to do something on the side." That can be a good way to get started in a new successful venture. Many people have started a part-time business and made it grow into a successful full-time venture. I would love to know the exact number of businesses that started this way.

There are all kinds of business ventures advertised. If you buy two hundred dollars worth of some training materials, you still have to have energy and motivation to put those training materials into a reality. Out of a hundred people who buy the training materials, I believe only a handful will be successful.

- When it comes to trying something new, there are at least three types of people.

- The first group will be those who will lose interest for various reasons or excuses.

- The second group will put out a little effort and will be moderately happy.

- The third and smaller group will put out the most effort because they want to be successful no matter what.

To be successful, you have to think hard. That means you have to study. That means you have to look for ways to outperform and to exceed in marketing beyond your competition. Even nonprofit organizations and museums have to think in new ways because they are in competition for the contributors' dollars.

- Lesson: If you think negatives all the time, you will deplete your emotional bank account.

The way people think makes a big difference as to how successful they are. If a person only thinks in terms of doing the basic acceptable work between 9 to 5, that person is too secure in the box and will likely fail to conceptualize a life or career outside the box.

On September 11, 2001, a lot of people lost their jobs through no fault of their own. When things are at their worst, we may be forced to take action and start over. Yet, in the midst of the worst situation, you may get a new concept that will improve your life. Anytime we are forced out of a comfortable job, we will have to look around for new concepts, which include possibly looking for a new job.

The downturn in the economy after 9/11 forced millions of people to rethink what they do for work and to conceptualize what new opportunities they may have to find for themselves. In fact, we should always be ahead of the crowd because most people get so comfortable in the box they have no understanding how to conceptualize what to do next if they are out of work. There are new people who will be millionaires during the downtimes because they know how to conceptualize new opportunities for themselves or their businesses despite the bad times.

There are times a person has to "take a job" to keep from starving. In difficult times, you still need to be positioning yourself so that when the economy recovers you are in front of the pack. There is nothing like looking back and thinking, 'Wow! I left the pack way back there.' I would like to hear from everyone who has discovered new success and a better life after reading this book. I would even like to make a TV show about those who have found success and new adventures from reading this book.

Many people should write a book, but many people will not make the effort.

Many people should be successful, but many people will not make the effort.

- Lesson: Remember, a concept will help you see the next plateau, but putting out the effort gets you there.

My wife used to work in a hospital as director of staff development. As a registered nurse, she has to know all the different areas of nursing and their requirements because she has to teach all the new nurses, orient them to the hospital, and organize teaching programs. She works with 400 to 500 people in the entire hospital. In the programs, she oversees nurses teaching other nurses. After attending a training program, those involved have to do an evaluation on each other and the patients. The written report provides a way to "complete the loop." This may surprise you. Do most people complete the loop? I don't think so. Someone leaves something out of the loop. What is left out of the loop in a hospital can hurt or kill a patient. What you leave out of the loop in your business can destroy your business.

I guarantee you that Bill Gates, founder of Microsoft, is sure to complete the loop in his business and make sure nothing is forgotten. The successful people are the ones who complete the loop. They make sure things run correctly and the right information is put into the system.

Why not think a bit harder to improve yourself and your success opportunities? When you get up and start a new day, you have to use your brain all day. By thinking creatively about new opportunities for yourself and your business, you can make a greater success happen.

This book is meant to get you to the next plateau, then the next plateau, and the next. Once your start thinking about new concepts to improve yourself or your businesses, you have already reached a new plateau. Once those new concepts grab hold of you, you will want to implement them. You will experience a whole new motivation about life and what you want out of life.

After reaching a new plateau, you then need to expend the effort and energy to establish the plateau as part of your life. The effort and energy can require you to make big sacrifices in order to be successful. When success is too easy, you may not be at your highest plateau.

Human beings are creatures of comfort. You may have to get beyond your comfort level and push yourself to think harder and to work harder.

People with plans are people who want to complete the loop. Someone like Bin Laden is out to complete the loop because, whatever you think of him, he is on a mission. He will make certain to do what is necessary to change history and to make the western countries do what he wants them to do. People can have a desire to achieve something for good or bad purposes. It is too bad Bin Laden did not build better hospitals and schools in Afghanistan, instead of choosing to go to war with the other nations and his fellow countrymen.

Societies with Mental Boxes

There are closed societies that could be improved by allowing their citizens to think outside the box. Some countries try to keep their citizens so restricted for political or religious reasons that the society remains poor and stagnant. There are countries and cultures that actually prefer people not to think outside the box. Women in some of these societies have not been allowed to have an education. In most democratic countries, women have used their freedom to speak out to accomplish greater equal rights. The hope is that closed societies will realize that democracy and freedom can create a better country. Not only that, most citizens in these closed societies desire better lives and the opportunity to be more successful. A country is improved when men and women have equal opportunities to be successful. As in no other country in the world, the great American experiment in freedom and democracy has proven for more than two hundred years that people want opportunities to improve themselves and that those improvements result in a greater, more dynamic country.

Just as societies need to be free and open for the free flow of ideas and information, you need to keep your own mind open to the free flow of ideas and how you can change your life.

- Lesson: The knowledge of how to work the concept is more important than worrying about making the money.

You may have a concept and to reach your next plateau you may feel you need a financial partner. You should try to see how far and how fast you can work your concept before you have to bring in a financial partner.

- There are people willing to work for free with your concept in order to be involved as employees or partners when your venture does start making money. This can be called the volunteer plateau.

Your concept may be so good you inspire other to work with you. They believe in you and *your concept* to the point of helping you for free. In return, they want to become successful too. If you use one person's help for free, you have to be a fair person. You have to *respect people* and *help those who are helping you.* You should want others to get something better for having helped you. By helping your volunteers to get what they want, you will help get what you want.

The volunteers could provide the *synergy,* where the results are greater than your individual talents. Having others helping you with your concept provides a *camaraderie*, too, that you would not have by working alone.

If you are not willing to help others, do not ask them for their free help. There will be a time when those who helped you as volunteers need to be reimbursed.

Some projects will excite and inspire different types of people. When I started the pizza business, there were two young men who wanted to help me get it started. Now, I know that most people do not want to own a pizza shop, even if someone gave them the money to get started. That is the point: you have to be honest about what you want or you will fail. If you are not excited about a great concept for a pizza shop businesses, then don't go into the pizza shop business.

On another occasion, I was working to develop the concept for a TV show. I did not have the capital to pay everyone to begin taping the sample show. I wanted to have as much of the show organized as possible before I considered financial partners who I feared could change the format of the show. There are times when you will get the free help from a lot of people, but remember to help them when your concept has turned into a success.

With just the concept of the TV show, I was amazed how many people volunteered. Of course, they were volunteering because they saw career opportunities for themselves and that is okay.

- Lesson: If you worry too much, you can become too negative in your thinking.

Most people worry, "I don't have the money." Probably ninety-nine percent of the people who have good or great concepts do not have the necessary money to get started. In my case, changes came about and I could not continue with the idea of the show.

If that is your situation, do not stay frustrated. Take your concept to the volunteer plateau. Assure those who help you that they can participate as employees or partners.

- Lesson: Think of the volunteer plateau as the way to get you and your concept ready for the investors plateau.

If people believe in you and your concept so much that they are willing to work for free, that should give you new *determination* that you can be successful. It is extremely rewarding when you know people believe in you. You are establishing your character and reputation to help others who believe in you.

Having the free help of others will likely *speed up* the time it takes to bring a concept into a reality. The speed of success may depend on having as many volunteers or paid employees as possible.

Your volunteers will likely have their own *expertise* and *experiences*, all of which should significantly improve your concept. Your are not expected to have all the answers, so let the knowledge and wisdom of others take your concept to the higher plateaus that you could not reach on your own.

The fact you and your volunteers are *hoping* for the project to be successful creates momentum to make something successful.

Module (Factory-Built) Homes

While running one of my businesses, I had extra time on my hands. I started looking around—outside the box. I saw an opportunity in module homes.

I started buying land and preparing to sell houses on the land.

I saw that most module houses were coming out of Pennsylvania. I thought, *that's where the herd is going. Why do I want to go there? Can I get module houses at a better price.?*

The module home developers were paying about forty-five thousand for a house. I went to Canada and got a module home dealership. I got the houses for about twenty-two thousand.

When the stock market crashed, I had to fold the cards and get out of the module home business. Over the years, I had built a number of module homes on Long Island.

Think outside the box in order to compete better with your competitor.

- LESSON: A business or an industry is never going to stay the same.

The economy changes, which constantly forces changes on industries and businesses. Consider the cell phone business. When cell phones first came out, I remember paying $1,500 for a cell phone. Now you can probably get a cell phone with a three-dollar coupon in a Cracker Jack box. A friend of mine who owned a number of cell phone stores and had connections to Nynex decided to fold his cards. He sold his business for $12,000,000. He felt his stores were becoming passé and he would not make enough money in cell phones as a small businesses owner. He still believes he made the right decision and he did.

I saw my auto reselling business starting to change and not be as profitable as it once was. That is when I had to be honest and look at my long-term goals.

The business was changing for two reasons. First of all, I had made such a name for myself that everybody was starting to try to do what I was doing. Secondly, the industry was changing rapidly. As it became more difficult to make money, I was positioning myself for a new opportunity. It did not matter that I did not stay in that businesses. My thinking never kept me stuck in the box.

I closed the auto reselling business. In the end, I had made real money, not just a living and I still own the shopping center on the property today. I knew I would be successful in my next adventure.

Chapter 8

Be a Good Listener

I call being a good listener a "tool" because listening to the *right* people plays an important part in becoming successful. If you do not listen to the *right* people, you could be left without enough information, misled, confused, or worse, on your way to failing. Whenever I think about getting into a new business, there are a couple of things I immediately do.

Step One: Collect All the Information

I usually start by touring the Internet to get a vast amount of new information. At first I shied away, but now my son points out that I've got the Internet bug like so many other people who surf the Internet. Once you're comfortable with the computer and the Internet, you can find so much information. With the powerful search engines available, I learned I could type in a subject and get thousand of pages of related information sources. Doing this amount of research could keep me awake for endless hours.

- Lesson: Never give up collecting the **knowledge and tools** that you need which will help you to be more successful.

Now, the Internet is not going to give you all the information. I know there are still books that I need to read at the library, so I have to "go to the library" on my list of things to do. One good thing about a free society: you have access to all types of books to help you do your research. America is what I call a "learning society" because we always want to learn more in order to do or accomplish more.

Even by reading, you are being a **good listener**. You are absorbing information that can help you. The same concept holds true for the Internet—you are finding out information from others.

Step Two: A Local Chapter

I look for a local chapter of people involved in a particular business and attend their meetings. Why? The key here is to network. There is a local chapter or local professional club for just about any field of interest. I find that at these meetings about one-third of the time is for socializing, one-third for networking, and the rest of the time for giving back to the community. While attending these clubs or meetings, I want to find out who the successful people are and what are their secrets for success.

By talking and networking with three or more people, you will gain new confidence in your endeavor as you share ideas. Even if you know how to put something together by yourself, you may still need that final expert to help you do what you want to do in a better way.

Step Three: Attend a Convention

I find out when the conventions for that business/industry are being held so I can attend one or more of them. If the convention is in Las Vegas, that's where I have to go because I want to learn what is happening in that industry.

By being a good listener everywhere you go and by talking to people, you can find out a lot of valuable information from these sources.

In the home inspection business, people ask me for advice or to recommend a contractor to do something. I have a couple of referrals in my pocket I can give the people. I advise them, "Call these ten people." They ask, "Why so many?" I say, "You can hire me for two days by the hour to tell you what you need to know. But, if you call in ten contractors, you'll get a good overall picture of what you need to know for free." You may not get ten contractors to your house, but you would get the knowledge you need by talking with them.

The other night the comedian Jay Leno told the joke about a town that got flooded. The federal representatives came on TV to say it would cost thirty million dollars to fix the damage. He wondered how did they get that estimate so fast. He said he had been trying to get somebody to come over to put a new bathroom for four months, but only two contractors out of ten showed up.

If you get a salesman to come by, you may have more questions about his suggestions and the estimate. If a hands-on contractor comes by, be a **good listener**. You'll be picking up knowledge that you need. As for any estimates, get three and go for the middle one. It is always important to check with the Better Business Bureau to make sure any contractor is reputable.

The same holds true for seminars. I've gone back to seminars more than once for the same person. I learn new information each time, either because I listen better or the speaker has something new to add. it's all about gaining knowledge, knowledge, knowledge.

You need the tools to go from making $60,000 to making $600,000 a year.

If someone comes in with a pneumatic hammer, he can frame a house in a day, compared to someone who has only a hammer. The difference in the tools that you have can make a difference in (1) how successful you are and (2) how fast you become successful.

I became involved in the American Society of Home Inspectors. We have monthly meetings where speakers come in to share their knowledge. That's a trade networking organization.

The more **knowledge** you can gather the more you will feel confident and be better prepared to do business. Successful people never stop learning. Of course, there's a curve where it gets to the point where you're not going to learn as much. However, I believe that, when you stop learning, you become bored. That's the time you should be doing something else.

Networking with trade organizations or any special-interest organizations can have tremendous rewards. Those networks have helped me to learn and to expand my business.

- Lesson: You have to keep learning in order to accomplish a higher level of success.

- Lesson: You have to roll the dice to be in the game.

The Value of Conventions

What you get at a convention are seminars and the ability to meet all the vendors. If you walk around a convention center a few days, you get new knowledge and get charged up to come back the next year. You should attend the seminars, even if you think you know everything and are already committed to getting started in that phase of the industry. During the seminar, you might find yourself pleasantly surprised because you had a misconception of a particular situation or item in that business or industry.

With a convention, you never know what you're going to find when you get inside.

I happen to know a young man who learned to buy four-family houses in New York with no money down. If he keeps going, he may be on TV some day teaching others the tools he has learned. Watch out for the wrong people who are eager to say, "It can't be done. It can't be done." They are most likely not the successful millionaires. Most things can be done, if you have the **knowledge.** Knowledge is more important to me than the money. If someone has the knowledge to buy a house without money, then you know that certain knowledge can be more important than the money.

- Lesson: The more you find out about your special industry at a convention the more tools you have.

Turns In the Road of Life

As a teenager, I discovered I could play a guitar and I got some satisfaction out of that. Also, I used to sing in a choir. Mixing the guitar and my singing lead me to singing with a band. I enjoyed not only inner peace from the music and singing, but I got satisfaction entertaining and connecting to an audience. My band was typically invited to come back to play again, and we were one of the hottest bands on a local level. I kept working with the band both full-time and part-time for about 12 years. After that much time, I began to realize something important: the odds of my making a good living in a band were against me, unless I became famous. I started out as a teenager hopeful of making it big, but I came to realize it was not forever. I had to get on another street to start making the bigger money.

I knew I was destined for something else. Back in 1970, I had gotten a real estate license with Berman Real Estate in Freeport, Long Island. I had the knowledge, but I did not feel ready to pursue a new goal or walk down that particular street at that time.

Interestingly, I had accidentally been making choices that had me weaving in and out of the construction business. I had been building modular houses in association with a supplier from Canada and took a turn in life to buy real estate.

In the next 25 years, I went through a number of other professions and businesses, but I kept coming back to real estate and real estate financing. I now network with thousands of people in the real estate industry and its related sub-categories: mortgages, home inspections, financing, construction, and government permits. My vast contacts have enabled me to see a cross-section of businesses, which means I see a lot of new opportunities.

I have a lot of knowledge about real estate, but I am the first to say I can always learn more. I keep honing in on any new knowledge that is important to my career in real estate.

Life is only so long. Every day you get older. Everyday you lose another day. The clock is ticking, even while you're sleeping. You have to work with your tools so that you can get to a point of success that the business takes care of you and you're not working an 80 hour week to take care of the business.

Kiwanis Club Is A Good Networking Group

In the mid 1980s, I joined a number of organizations. The one I stayed with was the Kiwanis Clubs, which is made up of local business people, who are either the business owners or the managers of a larger company. That club gave me any number of opportunities to meet high level executives and to **network** with the *right* people.

I came to find out that the people in the large corporations have the same problems as the small business entrepreneurs. The corporation is simply a larger business than the smaller one. Most of my peers are small business entrepreneurs, but keep in mind that small businesses really form the majority of businesses in the United States.

Dishonesty Does Not Pay

- Lesson: Be honest in business. Customers need to trust you and believe in you.

Now, we come to Enron—an example of the worst business people. Here were people calling themselves executives and wearing white shirts and ties, looking honest, but all the while they were more corrupt than your typical thief on the street.

I've found that there are three basic types of people in this world: honest, dishonest, and snakes. The *honest* person might tell a little "white lie" once in a while. The *dishonest* people I call the crooks. The crooks I can deal with because they pretty much let you know along the way that they are a crook. The problematic person is the *snake* who pretends to be honest and is just stealing out of your wallet.

A crook may get a couple of extra dollars faster, but it is not worth the loss of reputation or the risk of going to jail. Then what? The crook spends the rest of his life going around covering up what he did wrong. So what is the sense in doing something wrong? He could have taken that same effort and accomplished more positive things in life that will have greater results.

There are times when you are working on the edge, morally speaking. But when you take that step from the edge into the unethical abyss and the immoral, then you begin wasting your time by trying to cover up your lies and dishonesty.

- Lesson: Immoral acts in business distract you from your greater goals and can cause you to make wrong choices which can ruin your business.

Take McDonald's. Ray Crock, the founder, worked the concept and pleased the customers. Dave Thomas, the founder of Wendy's, was a man of high moral standards. Both were men with concepts and ambition.

Dealing with something illegal is thinking small. If a transaction is illegal, your name is likely going to come up with the police or the media. Dishonesty only destroys a business and a person's life.

- Lesson: Participating in questionable activities has killed many a business and many a career.

Business Never Stays the Same

I have always looked at other people's businesses. I have a friend of mine, Bob, who is a printer. He and I both are members of Kiwanis. With the advent of the computer, people can print business cards, letterheads, and many of the things this man has been selling for years. Bob is very creative and another one who believes in doing 110%. Bob is probably in his sixties. By now he does not have to work, but he takes it as a game. It is not a multi-million dollar business, but he has survived when other printers have gone out of business.

I see how Bob improves his business: He is always sending out a newsletter about himself and his business. He always has new ideas for expanding the business. He is always networking. He is always trying to forecast the future for his business.

- Lesson: The bottom line: Never stop **reinventing your business**.

There have been so many people that I have seen over the years who have learned to do their work at the one hundred and ten percent level. Some are more successful than others, but often those are the ones who are still learning the new knowledge to stay ahead of the competition.

In the music industry, a song on the radio that becomes a success has a hook to help people remember it. The hook can be the lyrics, the tune, the media coverage about the song, or the way it is promoted. Every business needs one or more hooks too. In my pizza business, I used the limo for delivery as a hook. In addition, I found Peter, who could create a great pizza sauce. The current owner still makes the sauce the same way we made it. The owner makes that 110% effort. The business is running quite well. One of the partners who took over the pizza business after me has moved in a new direction in his career. He felt it was time to move on.

Chapter 9

Consultants

Everybody cannot be experts at everything obviously. I can only tell you that I've used consultants.

What I have found is a consultant can give you a real overview of a situation of a business, just as counselors are consultants, too, who can help us get an overview of our relationships or our careers.

- The value of a good consultant is that you will be shown the pros and cons of what you are doing or need to do.

A nurse can explain to someone how to be a nurse, but the explanation will not be sufficient enough to open up a nursing agency. The person who opens a nursing agency has to understand the nurses' needs, the patients' needs, and what that business needs to work smoothly. A consultant can tie all this together.

If I wanted to open up a pizza restaurant, I would talk with the person who owns a pizza restaurant. He may say, "The help is terrible." I know because getting dependable employees became my biggest complaint.

As the business owner, you can make your own hours and you might expand the business into a catering business. The catering business may bring in hundreds or thousands dollars a year. By expanding into the catering business, you see more money coming in. On the other hand, you are faced with more problems. You may need more dependable employees, a greater line of credit to pay for your supplies, a fleet of delivery trucks, more insurance, more sales people to sell the services to the client, and so on. You become a very "needy" person to make sure everything operates smoothly.

- Lesson: Every business has its pros and cons. For example, out of a hundred people, maybe only three people are willing to make the commitment to the work that it takes to run a multi-million dollar catering business. The other 95 people will say they are not interested in *that* business or they don't want to work that hard.

If you went in and asked the pizza restaurant owner what he thought about the business, he most likely would start with his worst complaints. If the owner stays focused mostly on negative thinking, he will miss new and greater opportunities! That owner may need a consultant to see there are opportunities waiting to happen, such as opening a franchise business or moving his business to a new location where he could quadruple his income. Why is it that some business owners settle for a small business, while others grow into being a McDonald's? How are the people in the business thinking? Are they thinking big? Are they thinking positive enough? Are they looking for ways to expand?

If you asked a doctor, "What's your view on becoming a doctor?"

The doctor may reply, "Oh, do something else. The insurance and the health care system today are killing us. I have to have five employees on staff just to get paid." His complaints may go on about this and that. Does he tell you his positive side? Does he tell you about the apartment buildings that he started buying five years after he got out of medical school? Does he tell you he owns 20 buildings by now?

If you talk to someone about going into real estate sales, they may complain, "Oh, you have to wait six months to get your first check." Then, they'll start listing other complaints rather than focusing on making sales and buying property for their own real estate portfolio because that's where the real money lies in creating your future wealth.

- Lesson: Don't let people talk you out of doing something positive when you are ready to change and improve your life.

You have to be able to identify those who are only being negative and those who are giving helpful pros and cons. If you learn to be shrewd enough in real estate, you could end up like the other successful real estate developers.

A good consultant is going to give you the total overview that you need, not just the negatives. After all the advice, what happens in your life or your business still comes down to what decisions you decide to make and how venturesome you are willing to be.

I once paid a consultant to help me put on a craft fair. He gave me enough information that helped me to decide whether I wanted to put on a show.

What is in this book will stack the cards in your favor. I want you to succeed, but success is not done blindly. One of the goals of this book is to save you time and money. You can save time and money when you don't make <u>too many little</u> mistakes or <u>too many big</u> mistakes.

The Service Organizations Can Help You

Back in 1986, our Kiwanis Club wanted to put on a car show. Just because you like to drive a car doesn't mean you can put on a car show. Just because you like to stay in hotels doesn't mean you should open up a hotel. Just because you like to eat in restaurants doesn't mean you should open up a restaurant. My friend and I were car buffs in the custom car circle, but we still needed more help. We partnered with another Kiwanis club in Mamaroneck, New York, which has been putting on a car show for thirty years. Now, the connection with that Kiwanis Club provided us with their expertise about putting on a car show.

A group of us from our Kiwanis went up to Mamaroneck and had lunch with the other Kiwanis members who put on the car show. They were very specific about what had to be done. We were like puppy dogs. We just sat there, listening, taking it all in, and thanked them very much.

A car show is like holding a party, except for one major difference—not knowing the exact number of people who will show up. We found out there were a couple of ways we could lose money: (1) we could order too much food and not have enough people come or buy the food; or (2) we could pay a big price for the entertainment and not have enough people show up.

We had to learn: How do you prepare for this type of event?

We had to learn their formulas. One formula said: a specific type of advertising will yield a specific type of a response.

Other formulas were to be followed:

- For a car show, we needed cars.

- We had to mail an invitation to car clubs for people to bring their cars.

- We had to have judges, so people could be awarded plaques and prizes for showing their cars.

We wanted to get at least two hundred cars to show for the judges. Just as in a business, you think you have everything, but you cannot forget to put that garlic twist in the onion soup, as I mentioned in Chapter One.

We were concerned about how many people would attend with their cars. The Kiwanis Club members had told us that the preregistrations would account for fifty percent of the cars. Other cars would be brought to the show, as long as it turned out to be a nice day. From the advice, we hoped we would end up double the number of attendees based on how many people preregistered.

Two months before the show, we had only about twenty-five percent (or 50 people and their cars) registered out of our 200 car goal. A month before the show we got more registrations. All their formulas that they told us were working. And sure enough, we only had a hundred cars booked the day before the show. On the day of the show, 220 cars showed up. It was right to the formula.

Those other Kiwanis members were our consultants. Without their help, we would not have done as well. They did not have to spend a lot of time working with us. They simply gave us the formulas.

According to their formula, we picked a Sunday. We chose the second Sunday after Memorial Day. We added another aspect to the formula: we would do the show the same day every year. Over the years, people would know the show is scheduled at a predictable time, so they can plan their schedules in order to come back.

Without that knowledge of the formulas involved with putting on a successful car show, we likely would have made many mistakes that might have caused us to lose money.

- Lesson: Whatever you're going to do, you need to have the right **tools** and the knowledge.

You can't build a house with a broken hammer. The one who goes in with that pneumatic hammer is going to beat anybody else going in with a single hammer.

The same concept holds true for relationships. Just because you grew up in a family, may not mean that you know how to be a parent. You may have to learn many things: not to show favoritism for one child, not to neglect your children, not to fight too much, not to be a dictator and want everything your way, and to respect your spouse's needs.

A financial analyst always wants you to build your portfolio based on a pyramid formula. The stable stocks or investments are on the bottom. The risky or aggressive investments are at the top. The financial analysts are working with formulas that can work too. If you invest at an early age and continue to invest, you can become a millionaire when you retire. Young people should listen to these analysts and the formulas.

- Lesson: I always like to tell people, "Everything we're talking about is a guide."

That Galves Car Book was a guide when I had to buy cars at the auctions. That book became my basic guide. Then, I added my formulas. You need to develop more formulas that work for your business or your goals. At the auto auctions, my competitors were out there guessing and making big mistakes because they didn't have the additional formulas.

By the time I decided to move away from my car business, everybody else had started following my lead. They came to realize there were formulas they needed to learn from me. They used these formulas and were able to make more of a profit. Ironically, my competitors learned my unique business strategies. Wholesale met retail and took out the profit so it was time to move on.

Chapter 10

Long-Term Goals

Long-term goals are very important. People go through different stages and make accomplishments as they start out in life, such as graduating from school, or spending some time in the military service. Other people get married and start out on a career path.

Most of us make a good start at life in all these experiences, but then we get bogged down. We make it to a certain level, only to stay in the same cycle of routines and jobs. Some people stay in the same place because they want security and don't want to lose that regular paycheck. Some people may lack self-confidence because they have had bad experiences along the way with parents or friends, so they stay in their safe niche they have created to protect their feelings. They are afraid of criticism or rejection so much they are afraid to try anything new. Any negative comments from others become personal and painful, because they have not learned to let the negative attitudes and events in life roll off their backs. Some people are bogged down because they just don't know how to break away to reach another level. They need to develop new tactics, attitudes, contacts, and goals in order to move forward.

- Lesson: Those involved as owners and employees in business have to constantly develop new tactics, attitudes, contacts, and goals if it is to survive and be successful.

In business, I can honestly say, "The customer is not always right." However, you have to think of the consequences of having the wrong attitude about your customers. You and all your employees have to have this attitude: You make the customer think that he is right and think that he is a very important person (VIP).

The First Right Attitude: Under normal circumstances, the customer came into your store or business because he wants to accomplish a goal. He wants something, even if it is to return an item. He wants to accomplish a goal with the least number of problems.

The Second Right Attitude: The customer wants attention. Train your employees to be prepared to give the customer a lot of attention. How do you feel when a waitress takes your order, brings your food, and then is never seen again? You want more coffee. You want more bread. You want a new napkin. We've all asked the question, "Where's the waitress?" We've all had that experience where the waitress disappears and we're talking about disappearing forever. You may spend your whole life in the restaurant and she may never reappear. She seems to have gone into some black hole, either in the kitchen or out the back door. On top of that, the waitress wants a fifteen-percent tip for this service. Does the waitress reflect the attitude of the owner? One bad employee not doing the job the right way can hurt your business. More than one bad employee not doing their job the right way will destroy your business.

The Third Right Attitude: You make that extra effort to make a customer feel very special because <u>you are not just selling to that one customer</u>. Your customer is going to talk about your business. Your experience will be either positive and generate a lot of good publicity or it will be negative and, believe me, people will condemn you and your business into outer darkness, if they were not treated right. What are they doing? It may be called revenge. You treat them wrong and they are going to make sure everyone in town knows how terrible you are.

The Fourth Right Attitude: If your customer leaves happy, that customer will give you good word-of-mouth advertising. That's advertising that you don't have to put in your budget. It's free advertising. Those happy customers will tell people to run to your store. Those customers are willing to put their reputation on the line to make sure others know about you and how happy they will be.

- Lesson: People will give you word-of-mouth recommendations, if they like you. Word-of-mouth advertising is stronger and more cost effective than any radio, TV, or newspaper advertising.

If you get twenty new customers because you handled one customer the right way, you, not only make more money from the new customers, you do not have to spend money on advertising. A good reputation as a business is worth its weight in gold, as well as in saving advertising dollars. There are a few businesses that are actually able to keep getting new customers and never do any media advertising!

If a difficult person has been satisfied, then your business gets the reputation of being able to satisfy anyone who comes in. In fact, you may need to find out what the "word on the street" really is about your business. If people are expressing too many negatives, you have to move fast to make improvements or you may have to start getting ready to close your business—for lack of a good reputation.

- Lesson: Keeping one good customer happy could pay you back a hundred fold because the word-of-mouth will spread about your business to many other people.

Whether it's for yourself or your business, I tell people: set your goals in life. Now, nobody started off with a rowboat and owned an ocean liner two weeks later. You need six month goals, one-year goals, ten-year goals, and even a subset of goals during those periods.

Long-range goal setting I call "The Pyramid Step Method." You step up to successful accomplishments. Some people may never get to own the ocean liner, but they can enjoy what they're doing on their way up.

Two things are happening: (1) You are moving into new accomplishments and (2) you are learning some sort of happiness along the way. We know that not every day is the same in life. You may have a day when your car doesn't start. You may have a day when your dog gets sick and you have to take it to the veterinarian. You may have a day when you find out that the shipper cannot deliver the order for another three weeks. What are you going to do? Go crazy? No. You have to set goals and allow for problems and slowdowns to happen. They happen to everybody. If you are kicked back a few notches, you can always start over again and keep stepping up. Of course, you have to make your goals realistic.

- Lesson: There are times you will not be able to reach every goal. Sometimes, enjoying the ride is more fun than getting to the goal.

While this book is being written, I've been working on a new interesting endeavor. Just as I've done in the past, I'm using the Pyramid Step Method to develop the following: one month goals, two-month goals, six-month goals, one year goals, two-year goals, and five-year goals. Even though I have a lot of background in this particular field, there is still a learning period I have to go through. I'm adding a new twist, but that twist requires more learning.

Then the Second Phase will begin, but I need a couple of months to implement my new knowledge.

The third to fifth months will involve what I have to do to streamline this operation. Again, every new adventure and new road has its share of bumps, namely, mistakes.

The next two years I expect will require making the business work right.

By the third year, I will want to take the business to a new level. I envision all types of levels that I could take it to. But right now, I'm in the learning and the implementing stage, and all the new activity for reaching new goals is exciting. I'm taking each day at a time.

Writing this book is another adventure. I've gone through part of my learning curve. The next level is the implementing level. The implementing happens with my collaborator, Don MacLaren, who puts my words and thoughts into chapters. After we've prepared the book, we take it to the next level: getting it into print, marketing it in the stores and on the Internet as an eBook, and giving seminars on the information.

As in every business, it all comes down to the same thing: it's a matter of working according to formulas, taking the right steps, and going to the next level. Our ultimate level is reaching all the potential readers. Again, we would love to hear from the readers about what this book has come to mean to them.

- Lesson: Set your goals high enough to reach them at one level. Then go on to set new goals that will keep taking you to new levels.

There   are   plenty   of   national   statistics   about

businesses that fail. Always have contingency plans so you can survive the problems that will inevitably come along. With the right plans, the right attitudes, and the right goals that are realistically attainable, you will gain self-fulfillment seeing your business or career become successful.

Chapter 11

Position Yourself

You've always heard about the right time and the right place. Luck, sometimes, plays a part. But, you can get yourself beyond luck by positioning yourself.

First, you always have to surround yourself with sharp people if you're going to get ahead. If you were going to do something in country music, I would tell you to hang out in Nashville, Tennessee for a while. If you want to be an iron worker, you would have to immerse yourself in the unions, especially in the big cities with major development and sky scrapers being built.

Second, sometimes you can get stuck in a job, either as a very talented person or by getting stuck behind bosses who have ulterior motives. There are always ways to get out.

Third, if you're not positioned right in business, you may not see the proper side of that business. You may only see the negatives.

- Lesson: It's very important to get a balance in your life.

Very early in my adventures through life, I was living in California for three years. I was working as a auto bodyman on commission in a auto dealership. I found that I could never get any ahead in my career because I was always getting held up waiting for the parts. But I looked around and saw what was happening in the paint department.

The big paint truck would come everyday and deliver all the necessary paint. I decided that I was going to do the paint end of the body work. I moved into the paint department and proceeded to be probably one of the fastest and quality painters in Southern California. I know that because I had to put in my work slips when I was done. People from the factory came down because they didn't think I was painting the cars. They asked me, "How did you figure out how to do this so fast?"

I said, "I went to your one-day school. Nobody else took the time to go to learn how to do the job better. Then I had a rep from the factory come down and watch me work, because I began doing more warranty repair than any other technician. I was doing the work of five painters." He watched me and said, "Wow, did you get lucky! I see all the cars are the same color and that helps your speed." I said,

"That's not luck. I had gone down to the service writers and gave them the dates on a calendar with the paint codes so I would have those colors prearranged in the paint gun. They would get all the same color cars to come in on those assigned days, which make my system faster and more profitable."

Another time I was in the right place to meet another car buyer at a car auction. He offered me a position. I was in the right place at the right time. I met Joe. That helped me to take my income and my career and my knowledge to the next level. In two years, I was ready to open my own business called Northeast Liquidators company.

- Lesson: If your learning curve has stopped, get off the train and get into another more positive position.

Chapter 12

The Forest and the Trees

At this point, you are probably asking, "What's this all about?"

Well, let's look at a business. "The Forest," meaning the overall business model, looks good. The business seems to have good timing, good profit margin, good location, and a lot of good things going for it. Things couldn't be better for this business. If it's your business, you may have worked day and night to get the business operating smoothly.

Now come "The Trees," meaning the internal workings of the business. You have learned how to plant trees, harvest trees, sell trees, and ship the trees. By this time, you're an expert and you've been working with the trees so much that you might even think that you invented the trees (joke).

Just as a forest can suffer significant damage by floods, fire, volcanoes, and other natural events, businesses can suffer losses through natural events or when customers stop coming to that business and start doing business with the competitors.

- Lesson: Business constantly change. Fads come and go, and trends change, so you have to always adapt your business to the changes that are coming your way. For example, the fashion and automobile industries are actually in business to create change through new styles and new looks every year.

Probably many of us started out hating the computer and were slow to accept it, but all of us have had to adapt ourselves to using a computer. We have all become more technically sophisticated by using the computer and all the other electronic equipment that has become part of our lives. Whether in business, life, or relationships, there are internal and external forces changing us, our business model, career field, or relationship. Once the telephone was invented, the telegraph operators were a dying breed.

Listening to Some Real Estate Advice

This brings up a story related to real estate, and I have come to enjoy real estate as one of my best business adventures. Back in the 1980s, I was building and selling new homes. Also, I "land banked" many spot lots all over Long Island. That means, I got the permits to build and then waited for the right time to build. I eventually had a number of lots ready to build on when the stock market crashed. It became known as Black Monday in October, 1987. A successful developer said to me, "You had a great run, Les. Don't build on them, but sell them as lots with permits ready to build."

I could sell the lots and make a good profit, rather than build the houses and wait for the market to return. I followed the developer's advice. On the last piece of land I sold, the builder built a home, but he didn't sell that home for seven years. In this case, the builder did not see the down side coming in the market! He was too busy building the houses (the trees) and blinded by his optimism to see that the market (the forest) was on fire. In reality, there was not enough money available for people to buy homes.

Looking Through New Eyes

A successful chain store owner told me, "I have my manager go out every day and come back into the store, but he has to come in looking at things in the store with the eyes of the customers. Sometimes, he would see dirt on the windows. Another time he would see garbage in the parking lot. Another day he would see a crooked sale sign in the window." He had developed the "eye of the customer," and was not blinded by his own attitudes.

- Lesson: When you start looking at your business from the eyes of the customer, you will see things clearer than you ever saw before.

There are people who will not reach their goals. The forest may look good at first, but some people may not plant the right seeds (for a multitude of reasons), so that forest will not become larger and healthier. Some people will get bogged down with the trees around them and not see the whole concept (forest) and how to improve it.

The goal here is to look at your own life and career, including the success of other people's lives, careers, and businesses, in order to gain a clearer image of what needs to be done for yourself and your goals.

I have found that I have to look around me at what is happening in society, a specific business, or career field. It's interesting to note that one of the wealthiest persons in China is a woman, Yan Cheung, who made her billions with paper manufacturing (*Forbes* Billionaires, March 26, 2007). She ranks 5 on the list of 400 richest Chinese. Despite the electronic and computer age around us, people in China still need a lot of paper. She saw the need for paper (the forest) and how to apply the trees to that great social need. She literally applied the forests and trees of the world to provide for the paper needs of China and became a billionaire. Obviously, her success proves that the world is not made up of "paperless societies" and that societies will always need paper in one form or another.

- Lesson: You should be constantly analyzing different situations and using creative marketing every day in order to be more successful.

A lawyer friend of mine got mixed up in the political arena. He soon backed away because he saw that by the time he would be in a place where he could change things, he would owe too many favors to too many people and that bothered him. He felt he would not reach some of his idealistic goals. The forest looked good at first, but he felt he would not be able to plant the right seeds. In other words, others would be telling him what seeds to plant and controlling what happened in the forest because of political favors owed to them.

Each forest in the world serves a different function in nature and has to be treated differently. For example, the rain forests are vastly different from the forests of England, Europe, or Russia. Whether in business or relationships, people, sometimes, can get distracted by all the "trees" around them, which makes them forget the concept of the whole forest and what is special about that forest.

- Lesson: Competitors are constantly changing the world around us, so we must look around for opportunities and keep improving our business model or career path all the time.

Those of us who live in modern western societies know the importance we put on research that will lead to new changes and improvements. As a people, we seek to know what is new and better for at least two major reasons: (1) to make our lives better and (2) to make a profit. For example, improvements are constantly being made in medicine, but, again, for reasons one and two. The pharmaceutical industry comes out with new drugs, but, again, for reasons one and two. Architects design creative building styles, but, again, for reasons one and two. The architects want us to appreciate their creativity in designing beautiful eco-friendly buildings, but their buildings must have tenants (profit motive) or the owners will go bankrupt if tenants do not occupy that building. Since we live in an ever-changing society, we must adapt ourselves and our businesses to the fast-paced changes coming our way, while maintaining excellent quality control of our business (healthy trees make for a healthy forest).

Chapter 13

Be on the Right Street and Walk

New York City's Mayor Michael Bloomberg is said to have spent about $50 million to get elected. As great as his accomplishments are, you have to remember that he has to put on his shoes and get his coffee and orange juice every morning just like the rest of us. If he was playing Monopoly, he would be on Park Place, while most of the world is on Baltic Avenue.

Everyone has personal problems. Nobody has that golden life that everybody thinks someone else has. Yet, we all strive to achieve a golden life.

Over my years in different businesses, sometimes, I've been on the right street and, sometimes, I've been on the wrong street and I've had to change my direction.

Small Business versus Big Business

I've found that the smaller the business the more "hands on" I had to be in order to make it work. Although you may have more control, a small business or profession can be very labor intensive of your own time. Even though you don't have thirty employees and hundreds of items, the whole operation is all on your shoulders. A simple thing as a few days vacation may be impossible to take.

When I had my larger business, Northeast Liquidators, it had many moving parts, but, since it was lucrative, I was able to pay people more money. By paying better, I was able to get better people. I always found that I didn't want super star people. I wanted a good employee because a good employee I could make a great employee; if I paid them a little bit more. A friend of mine told me that there is a theory in a book on who to hire and how to pay them, but I can tell you what I know that works. I estimated that I might be paying my people about a third more than other businesses were willing to pay. However, I didn't need twenty-five employees at lower salaries, I only needed twelve employees. The difference: I had twelve happy employees, instead of twenty-five unhappy employees not making enough money.

I also found that I had more personal free time with

that larger business. Of course, free time for most people means going off on a vacation. For me, my "free time" meant looking on another business adventure. This time I started getting into module homes. While the other home developers went to Pennsylvania to find out about module homes, I went to Canada. I found the module homes were less expensive and were built better.

- Lesson: You have to decide what street you want to walk on.

With a small business, problems can come up and all those problems can eat into your time. With a large business, you're able to pay good money to get qualified people who can spend their time to solve the problems that come along.

- Lesson: Good pay is one main point for getting and keeping good employees.

The Right Employee

I found that a good worker to me was not necessarily a worker that had a tremendous amount of training. It all boiled down to *attitude*. I can teach anybody almost anything, if they're willing to listen and have the capacity to learn.

Some people are stuck in a rut. They can be problem employees because they keep doing things the same way and very seldom try to change. Some people will work with little motivation. We can see what an average person accomplishes.

If you give some people goals as to how to make more money, they usually will be your better employees. If someone can peel a hundred potatoes a day, you can give them a goal to peel one hundred and twenty-five potatoes and increase their pay to one hundred and twenty-five percent pay, based on reaching that goal. This concept is almost like putting the person on commission. People on commission always have incentives and are always better workers than the ones that aren't on commission.

If you can get a janitor to sweep faster or work better, you can have an arrangement to pay him more.

Incentives can have good payoffs for both the employee and the business. As an employer, you may have to start asking yourself: What incentives are you adding for your employees? What new incentives do they want to have? Are you willing to accommodate them or will your employees go somewhere else?

Most employees have some simplistic goals: how many days can I get off? How can I extend my lunch time?

Take the same people who put all that effort into trying to figure out how not to work and tell them you will work out a plan with them to help them make extra money, then you have a chance for making good employees better.

Some employees may not improve. Some people are not goal-orientated. Those employees you may have to get rid of or keep them in their mundane jobs. Some people get into a security cubbyhole and only want to stay there. They are not ready, not able, or are afraid to think outside the box.

Changing Employees into Better Employees

If you can make an employee become more goal-orientated and you give the person a new monetary incentive, you might get double the work out of someone who has the motivation.

The concept of goals and money incentives is what separates the men from the boys. The men will go after the opportunity, the boys won't. Some people would rather be boys and not be motivated. If you don't want to change or to improve your life, you should get your money back because you're not ready to move ahead.

The lessons in this book are about personal goals, the right attitude, and how anybody can learn to have a better life.

When you have the attitude of "I want to accomplish more" then this book will help you find ways to get to the next level if you are on the right street.

Chapter 14

Seminar Selling

Sears & Roebuck became a successful retailer by selling items through a catalog. That was a milestone in retailing because it expanded their customer base when people could not get to the store and it expanded the variety of items they could sell.

Today, if you want to buy something, you go on the Internet. My wife lost some directions about repairing something. She went on the Internet and found the directions about repairing a light switch in the house. The Internet means we have expanded our way of selling today.

Seminars: A Way of Selling

I found that I could make a business out of seminars. I found it very helpful to expand my business by conducting seminars. You can use seminars to educate people about a product or a service that you are selling.

- Seminars become one of my tools that I have used in just about all my businesses.

In a seminar, I can educate 25 people at a time! To make the seminar educational, I don't end by saying, "If you want to buy this or that, come up." I give the audience another option by saying, "If anybody has any more questions, I'll be in the back of the room for fifteen minutes."

That fifteen minutes turns into two-and-a-half hours of follow up questions. I have found that those who come up with questions turn into new leads. Then, you can proceed to turn them into sales.

Module Home Seminar

I call each of my new businesses "adventures." When it came to starting the module home business, I thought that all I had to do was to put a little ad in the paper that read, "How to build a module home. Free seminar."

I rented a hall at a Holiday Inn. At that time, we were referencing the business names of those who did home foundations because the module homes came in pieces. We still needed contractors to do all the side work.

I had about four hundred pictures and I was able to put together a seminar slide show. I thought I would get about 25 people. By the time of the seminar, I think I got about a hundred and twenty people to show up. Many of the men in the audience were builders who knew as much as I did, if not more. I thought, I'm really on the spot here.

I went ahead and did the presentation. At the end, I say, "We have a few minutes for questions. I'll be in the back to answer any questions." Out of the one hundred and twenty people, you want to get to the twenty people who are serious and who may want to do business with you. Those who come to the back are the ones who ask more in-depth questions. We did 17 sales from that seminar; we probably could have had more sales if the stock market had not crashed six months after the seminar in 1987.

It became a matter of **positioning** the business at the wrong time. The stock market will influence your business. A recession or an economic downturn can hurt most businesses.

In a prior seminar, we sold out the seating and, ultimately, sold about fifteen houses, which is quite impressive. When I held the seminar, I had to pay $300 to rent the room and provide pencils and notepads, while I had no guarantee I would sell any home.

Sometimes, sales people think only about paying for one lead. They never think about putting everybody in one room at one time. As long as the seminar tactic does not get too tacky, the more light-hearted the seminar, the stronger it is. You should not even have to ask for the sale; the sales come to you once you have gained credibility!

Home Inspection Seminar

When I was trying to build up my home inspection business, I put together a course for the American Real Estate School. The school offers continuing education to brokers because in New York State you need continuing education credits. <u>I got this program certified</u> so the brokers could use the course for credits. This allowed me to have a captive audience. I usually had about 15 people in the same room for seven and a half hours. I received a moderate amount of money that paid for the day.

The good part is that I wound up picking up customers. Not all of them called the first week, but just about everybody from the whole class called over the next year and a half.

Seminars selling can also be used as a teaching class.

My cousin is very successful in financial planning and tax plans. He used to give continuing education seminars to CPAs. He does not make a living on the seminars, but, when people get into a tough situation, guess who they call? They call him and he does a lot of high end referral work.

Positioning Yourself in a Seminar

I was at an Expo for new home buyers. They asked me if I would get up and speak on home inspections, which is one of my businesses. A major bank was the one promoting the event. There was a speaker for mortgages, myself for home inspections, and a third speaker. I had asked to end the seminar because I know from experience that the participants tend to remember the last speaker.

The first person rambled on, reading out of a book, which started me yawning. The second person was knowledgeable about appraisals and home owners insurance, and gave a hard sell.

As the last speaker, I got up and said, "I'm going to be ten minutes and I'm going over three points. I could go over a hundred points, but there are three points that are important."

First, the people knew they only had to sit there another ten minutes. That gave them a feeling of wanting to stay, so they would not start to leave.

Second, I was able to get across three very important issues about buying a home.

At the end, the host said, "If anybody has any questions, our consultants will be here afterwards."

I thought there was a problem. I didn't know what

was going on because I had a line of people waiting to ask more questions. I had captured the attention of all the people. The other speakers had a lot of great information, but it was rambling and incoherent.

I wanted to hit on three very important points and then I ended the seminar. The outcome is that I went on to inspect everyone's house that stood in line, except for about two people. This is the power of seminar selling.

- Lesson: Seminar selling is not really selling. It's being informative. People will come back to you because they want more help and because they trust you.

Basically, you have a lot of people in one room. They were interested enough to come to hear you or they would not be sitting there. It's up to you to make that seminar, informative talk, or educational day a good event.

With the Internet, television, catalogs, books, magazines, and newspapers, we have so much access to information. We live in an information age. Even with all the information on Google and the Internet, people still like to come together for special seminars in order to hear special information. I think there will always be a need for seminars.

Network Connections Always Count

To start getting connected, you may establish seminars through banks or real estate people who are advertising.

Whatever profession you're in, you should go to your Kiwanis or local networking service organizations. The deeper you get into these groups then you can start using all your tools. Sometimes, you have to give extra time networking. People who see you out there feel more comfortable to do business with you or to come into your store. You can't get anywhere sitting in front of the TV eating Bon-Bons or watching the sports channel all day.

Cy Sims, the clothing retailer, has made millions on his slogan: "An educated customer is our best customer."

As a reference, *Newsday* newspaper lists in the business section all the seminars in the area. It's very helpful to get yourself out there. The more you're out there meeting people the more new business will be generated.

- Lesson: Seminars are a lot better than cold calling because the potential customers are coming to you.

Years ago, I knew two partners in a very successful Chevrolet dealership who had started out as used car salesmen. They would never walk out to a customer. The customer always had to go to them. They felt that the customer was now coming into their arena. They proved to be very successful.

- Lesson: People have come to your seminar because they are already interested in obtaining something from you. You have to provide them with what they need, but leave enough unanswered questions so they will come to you for more answers at a later date.

In your presentation, get your points across very simply and don't be too wordy. Get to the point one, two, and three. Some people may have come a long way, so you may have to keep the meeting to one hour. You also need to plan an extra twenty or thirty minutes to speak to people after the meeting. I also encourage questions. It helps me to weed out my audience to find the serious people. There will always be those who say, "I'll use the information another day." Fine, let them go. That's the magic of a seminar that generates new sales.

If people are lined up to see you, it's obvious they are there because they're interested. If you really made a hit with the audience, you can tell them to meet you afterwards.

If you have a large audience, you always should do the

seminar with someone to help you with crowd control.

You don't want to tell the audience everything. You want to leave them with a couple of questions in their minds. You can determine how many customers you have or how many could be turned into customers by the number of people who want to meet you after the seminar.

You can travel to seminars as far as your product or service will reach. If you're selling a local service, you may be limited to a 50-mile radius.

Would I drive to North Carolina if I could make $5,000 for the day? I would, although I would not want to think it was for the money. If I have a book to sell, I could travel anywhere. When it comes to traveling, it's better to go to a highly populated area where two million people live, rather than go to a small town. However, it all depends on your market. **Market means how many people can buy a given product or service at a given location.**

If you don't have an idea what your market is, you should not be conducting a seminar.

I've used slides in seminars and overhead projections. The best is projecting an image against a wall using PowerPoint presentations. Everybody loves visuals and graphics during the presentation. The general rules are:

- You don't want to tire out the audience with too much information.
- You want to tell some stories and anecdotes to keep their interest.
- You want to keep the seminar light-hearted enough so the meeting does not seem like you're a barker at a medicine show trying to sell them snake oil.

If I had to sell snake oil, I would start by talking about the bottle and how the bottle was made. Then, I would talk about how the snake oil was made. I would get into facts, figures, and studies on how many snakes had to be cut up to be poured in there. By the time I got done, I would be teaching about the product. If you educate people about the product, the product will sell itself.

If you play the game right, the money will follow in the "game" of business.

It comes down to keeping it simple enough that people will get the point. You want to put just enough ginger in the food to flavor it. Too much ginger will kill the enjoyment of the food.

If you give people too much education about any particular thing, whether in a meeting or person-to-person, they may lose interest. Less information, but the correct information, is better than being over-informed.

When I do home inspections, I want to get to the point. Every house has a couple of loose screws in it. Sometimes, it's the owner with the loose screws. But every house has a downside and a few little problems here and there. If you over-emphasize the small stuff, they're going to get lost. Meanwhile, I don't want the buyer to forget the fact that they need a $5,000 new roof or a $3,000 boiler.

When you're trying to direct people, you **don't want to weigh down the saddlebags of information** too much. You just want to give them enough so they get the point.

Attend a Seminar a Second Time

I've gone to a lot of seminars in my adult life. Sometimes, I'll go back to the same seminar a second time, even if it is the same speaker. Someone may ask me, "Why are you doing that?" I know the speaker is never going to approach the same information the same way. He is going to approach it from a different angle. This approach helps me gain new ideas.

Also, give out business cards or little pamphlets. I don't believe in giving out big books.

A sales person will go to someone's home and take an hour and a half to pitch the sale. I prefer to bring people together and use only 50 minutes to pitch the people and provide time for follow-up questions. I could end up with half the audience calling me. That hour and a half can turn into thirty sales instead of one sale in a home.

Sample Pizza Business Promotion

If you conduct seminars, they have to be promoted because every business needs promotion. Instead of giving you a seminar promotion story here, let me give you a story about promoting our pizza restaurant. When we opened the restaurant, I wanted everybody to taste the pizzas. It cost me two dollars to make a pie, which included the cost of the box, cheese, and other ingredients. I would pick Monday or Tuesday nights, which were our slower nights. I would advertise the pizzas for $1.99 each between 5 and 7 'o clock. I don't remember the exact number, but we would sell at least 200 pizzas in those two hours. We had people lined up outside the door and down the block. It was a great promotion. How else are you going to get everybody to taste that pizza? People were saying, "Hey this tastes great." We made our pizzas with a sesame seed crust.

Those promotions put our restaurant on the map. It definitely worked. Somebody may ask, "Why are you giving that all away?" I'm not giving away anything. Maybe I'm not making money for those two hours. But, by selling 200 pies, instead of ten, I had the opportunity to make new customers.

You have to test your market with a promotion. I tried to give away free tires in my tire business. People did not believe me. They must have thought I was selling inferior tires, only one person came. It shows you that some promotions may not work, if people are afraid of something.

If I still owned the pizza restaurant, I would keep running the $1.99 pizza promotion once a month. Just to test the market and gain new customers. To have 200 people sampling your product at one time is a unique type of seminar that provides samples to all that attend.

Chapter 15

Live Below Your Means

After you figured out if you have *blind ambition,* after you did your *homework,* after you learned how to be a *good card player,* after you became a *good listener,* after you took time to c*onsult* with others, after you set your long-term *goals* in order, after you learned to *position* yourself and stay on the *right* street, you now have to learn to *live within or below your means.*

If you have an income of $5 million, you can still be foolish and spend $7 million on a boat or other expensive luxuries, if you let your success get out of control and make the wrong choices.

I believe that the fun and enjoyment of going through life is making good things happen in life. All of us need time to relax and enjoy the ride, but I do not recommend overspending on luxuries or overindulging yourself.

I read a story about a person getting on a train and the

train kept stopping at the local stations. Another person got on the express train and boom! In a short time, the ride was over fast. However, the person who took the local train got to see more at each station and enjoy more.

- Lesson: By living life in the fast express lane, you can miss out on seeing and learning about a lot of the things along the way in life.

The other story I heard was about children. Wishing the child can sit up, that's good. Wishing the child can feed itself, that's even better. Then you wish for the child to go to school so you can have two minutes to yourself. After that, you can't wait for the child to get through high school and college. It becomes a matter of wishing your life away. The age old advice to slow down and learn to enjoy life is still very good advice.

- Lesson: The rush to be successful will not automatically make you successful any faster.

A zealous, frantic pace can lead you faster into the hospital and may defeat your plans to become successful. Just a couple of weeks ago, my wife said to me, "You have a stint in the hospital every two years from trying to accomplish too much and do too much. You better put the brakes on because every time you get into the hospital your health status becomes compromised." She should know because she's a nurse educator! I have to admit my wife approaches opportunities totally different than I do, but I also need to listen to my wife's advice. As someone once said, "You don't want to end up in the grave today because you wanted to be the richest man on earth."

Everybody needs a check and balance system. Successful people seem to get caught up in a race and they just keep running.

I have mentioned about inner peace and think that *inner peace* is a measurement of success. Making money is only part of the measurement of success. In fact, money is too often overemphasized as a measurement. *Forbes* likes to make an annual list of billionaires. There is no success list based on those who have found inner peace. Mother Teresa would certainly have qualified on the inner peace list, but she certainly had no desire to be on the billionaires list. Jesus taught in the Beatitudes, "Blessed are the poor in spirit, for theirs is the kingdom of heaven." (Matthew 5:3 NIV) No one especially likes to be poor, but maybe getting into heaven should be a measurement of success too, and money apparently is not necessary for getting into heaven or most of us would never make it there.

I am back to the need for a balance in life. If you

have $5 million dollars, it may not be in your best interests to spend all your waking hours trying to get to the next level, if you do not know how to enjoy the level you are on already. My cousin, Fred, who is a very successful financial high end consultant, said, "If you have $5 million, you can live comfortably in your remaining years."

- Lesson: The measurement of success in some ways is enjoying the level you have accomplished.

The majority of successful people usually have a plan in place. They reached a level that gave them enough money to be able to join the country club. They bought that new Bentley every two years because they knew they could afford it.

By the time they reached their forties or fifties, they have learned to live within or below their means. If they wanted to go on a $20,000 dollar Alaskan cruise for two weeks, they could afford it. Although their lifestyle is out of the reach of the average person, they have learned what they can afford.

You might be surprised to know that some wealthy people also go to McDonalds even though they can afford a gourmet restaurant every day.

- Lesson: The foremost financial lesson in life is this: Never out spend your money, and remember that the temptation to outspend is always there.

You don't want to buy anything expensive and then be left working to pay off your debts. You don't want to become a slave to your possessions or purchases. Instead, you want to make your life easier. You can make your life easier by using all the tools I spoke about in this book.

Each of you will take and use the tools in a different way. Eventually with a plan, you will wind up with some sort of success, happiness, and inner peace. The goal here is to help you find success, so that you do not work from nine to five for six days a week and end up at retirement time with a meager pension and living in poverty. Everybody has heard the old expression: work smart, not harder.

This book is a guide. It's meant to give you principles to work smarter. Some people just want to figure out how they can get out of work and go play golf every day. If that is your goal in life, I hope you can play a round of golf every day. You accomplished your goal and I hope you have inner peace.

Through my vast network of people in all my different careers, occupations, and organizations through life, I've always enjoyed studying people.

For example, I have a friend, who is single, very sharp, and was in the corporate world. He made a living, but he was more concerned with simply enjoying a stress free life. He is self-employed where he can work one week and take the next week off. Although he could do so much more, he is happy to make money this way. He's living at one end of the spectrum. There's a song by Kenny Loggins about winning all the money in the world and then losing your soul. Winning all the money in the world doesn't mean you are going to have happiness; all the money doesn't mean you are going to have inner peace. Luckily, this friend of mine had some success at inner peace. If you have found inner peace, that to me can be a measure of success too, even though others may not measure you as "successful" in their eyes.

I have another acquaintance of mine who is on a mission. I don't know what drives him. I would like him to read this book, hoping that he may realize that he should calm down and that the rush to success can have a defeating, even deadly toll on himself and those around him. He's a very talented businessman, but it seems he is on a mad mission to reach his success. I believe he can find both success and inner peace, but it may be more difficult for him to learn the inner peace attitude. The book's title says, "Making Money, Not Just A Living." Making money also means having enough money so you can enjoy life. God gave us two things to slow us down: (1) the need to sleep and (2) taught us to take one day a week for worship and rest. We are not programmed to work 90 hour weeks and to expect our employees to do the same.

It's interesting how my single friend is the opposite of my businessman friend who is driven to work so hard.

You may dream of making $5 million a year, but you have to have specific ways of making that amount of money.

- Lesson: Being driven to make money does not guarantee success. In fact, you may only exhaust yourself and not reach your goals.

Maybe the adventure is just too exhausting and it's not fun anymore. So, think of yourself in a boat. Sometimes, it is better to get out of that boat and jump into the lifeboat. From your lifeboat, you may be able to reflect on how you were going in the wrong direction. The good thing is that your lifeboat provides you with the means to get to another boat. Your new boat may be smaller, but you may find inner peace. As one man told me, "I'd rather be a big fish in a small sea than a small fish in a big sea." Everyone has his own level of where he should be.

When I was younger, I had way too much drive to want to succeed. But I didn't have enough tools to know how deep the water was in the pool before I jumped in. I managed to survive through a lot of mistakes. I probably made a lot more mistakes than I should have because I did not have the right tools.

Some people get knocked down in their careers and they can't get up. I was like Rocky in the ring, but I didn't know how to throw back the right punches. Before learning my important lessons from Joe, I only had the *drive* and the *blind ambition*, but not the right tools. Although Joe was ten years younger than me, he had the tools that I needed to make success happen.

Today, Joe has a sizable real estate development business and is doing very well. He sold the auto business, which had about a hundred people working there. I believe Joe has found success and *inner peace*.

The majority of us will not become the billionaires of the world, such as Donald Trump or Bill Gates of Microsoft. But there are always ways to make a million here and a million there, if you are clever enough to find a niche market and don't give up on yourself.

I also observed that Joe surrounded himself with sharp people. You have to think about your people who make up your business. They may be worth that extra money every year because you will be making double, triple, or more results than your competitor who boasts how cheap he can get people to work.

With all the money in the world, you can only eat one steak a night. If you eat two, you'll get fat and die sooner.

You may find yourself in the hospital and my wife the nurse educator may have to teach you some lessons! This is to say you can only do so many things each day. You need some sort of balance with your time so that you are not driven the wrong way, and possibly hurt others unnecessarily along the way. If you overwork too much, you could miss what it means to have inner peace. Many people are driven to make as much money as possible. There may be several reasons why someone is driven to make money: Greed and selfish concepts; competition with family or associates; desire to control everything about making money; or feelings of inadequacy of not having a certain amount of money.

You have to discover what is pushing you to try to be successful. It could be something that has lingered from your childhood. I think I tried to overcompensate for the learning problems I had in school by proving I could be successful, and more successful than most of my classmates.

I remember the difficulties I had in school. I could not pass the tests like the other students. I found out later in life that I did not have what is called "instant recall." If you ask me something, I know the answer, but it might take me longer to get the answer because parts of my brain are not connecting that fast. My teachers and I never realized my learning disability when I was in school. I only learned about it a few years ago. So, I overcompensated by having an overabundance of drive to push myself ahead. I was trying to overcompensate for my handicap without knowing what my handicap was at the time. All the other students could read part of a book and be ready for the test the next day. I needed more time to memorize what I needed to learn and to get ready for the test. On the other hand, I could build a shed in a day without any problems, while the test-oriented students could not build a shed in two weeks.

I realized that those who pass the tests quickly may not be any better than me at making money or being successful. In school, I certainly was not the most promising student to bet on who would turn out successful! But here I am because I have learned how to succeed a whole lot more outside of school.

- Lesson: Schooling is a good foundation. However, you have to apply the lessons in this book and what you learn in life to be able to build a skyscraper of success on your foundation.

The book is meant to be your architectural blueprint for building your skyscraper of success.

Real success means finding *inner peace* and your inner peace should help others to find inner peace too. If you don't have time for yourself, what's the sense of all the hard work? If you've been working and driving yourself for eight years without a break, *you need to take a vacation*! It's time to get away from the driven life and rethink what is important. What you discover during that break time will help you to live longer.

Overdriven people wear everybody else out around them. Others feel obligated to keep up. The wrong attitudes can destroy the goal to success because most people get burned out if they try to keep putting in many long hours.

I look back and think I should have had six children. I had only one son. That choice may have been my mistake. I could probably have had my children help me in my work just as our son has been part of my business adventures. We are all making choices year by year that affect our lives and careers. Our lives become the sum total of our choices. It may have been nice to have a larger family. On the other hand, all those children may not have gotten along. Most families have bumps in the road when it comes to raising children, so it may have been better just to have a small family.

- Lesson: The goal for each reader is to use one or more ideas in this book that will influence your life to be better.

Money often makes life easier. I've seen more marriages split up because of no money than those who split up because there was too much money. You can certainly get along with little money, if you have all the love in the world, but it is harder without enough money.

- Lesson: I recommend that you read this book twice because you will get new ideas each time you read it.

You will be helping yourself to improve each time you read this book. Also, you may know somebody who needs this book. Give them the book as a gift so that person will not miss a day making the same old mistakes. That's a true friend.

Through the years, people have said to me, "Les, you're a successful person. What does it take to be successful? I only have 5 minutes to listen. Well, my answer will not be in 5 minutes or less. This book proves that.

Now that the book is available, I would like to hear from every reader. I am especially interested in hearing from those who read the book and found it turned their lives around. This book can be a guide and help you about thinking a whole new way so that you can find better ways of living and working. You can reach me by email. By sharing comments with others, everyone will get ideas that will be more valuable than any money payment. The goal of helping you and other readers will help me reach another higher level in life. Through this book, I will be helping so many people find inner peace. It is important to me to help you get to the next level and accomplish something better in your life.

After the book is published, I'll enjoy holding seminars to discuss new ideas based on this book. I'll also enjoy meeting with you and your friends. In a way, I hope the final chapter of this book will never be written because I will probably be on to another new adventure, which will be worth another chapter!

REIEC Is a New Adventure

As for now, I have been focusing on an REIEC (Real Estate Investment Education Club). The club has two goals: exchanging real estate knowledge and helping people to achieve some of their real estate goals. We have meetings once a month, seminars, and subgroup meetings. Whether a person is a beginner or an expert in a real estate-related field, people have the benefits of networking and meeting qualified speakers who will educate them in the difficult facets of real estate investment.

Let's take real estate and do a broad stroke of the brush as to what REIEC is trying to do:

Kindergarten

>   Begin your research

Grades 1-6

>   Buy, flip, and hold real estate

Grades 8-9

>   Holding to Build Equity

Grades 10-12

>   Commercial real estate versus apartment and
>   residential

Bachelor's Degree

>   Retail, Stores, Office, Apartment,
>   Commercial Investment Buildings, and
>   Developing sub-divisions.

Master's Degree

>   Power strips, outlet centers, and
>   manufacturing facilities

Doctorate Degree

>   Building towns and malls

I have been involved in many facets of real estate. Some I liked and some I didn't like. I always wanted to do better, so I kept on learning more and more because I needed the tools. In real estate, I've been involved in a shopping center and commercial projects. I can speak on many facets of real estate and share my unique experiences. A lot of what I have accomplished I could not have done without my wife. As a husband and wife team, we hope to take the club to another level. How long will it take to reach such a goal? I don't know.

I'm reminded of the story about taking the train ride to the next station. At this point in my life, I'm interested in enjoying the ride to the next station. If I reach the next station by taking REIEC to another level, all well and good, but I still feel I have already found inner peace at this time in my life.

I hope you have enjoyed the ride (the book). Also, I hope you use this knowledge well. The lessons in this book I have used and preach in my everyday life and feel that the lessons have helped me all the way.

Stay Tuned There's More Coming

Hey, hey! Something just happened.

I just had another idea.

Another light bulb just went off!

I just got the title for my next book: "Making Money, Not Just A Living in Real Estate."

I look forward to seeing you at one of my seminars.